THE GIRL IN THE GREEN JUMPER

GREEN JUMPER

My Life with the Artist Cyril Mann

For Amanda, our brown-eyed baby

Pimpernel Press Limited
www.pimpernelpress.com

The Girl in the Green Jumper
© Pimpernel Press Limited 2022
Text © Renske Mann 2022
Photographs © see page 175

A catalogue record for this book is available
from the British Library.

ISBN 978-1-910258-51-4

Typeset in Kis Classico
Printed and bound in China
by C&C Offset Printing Company Limited

9 8 7 6 5 4 3 2 1

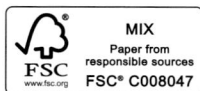

MIX
Paper from
responsible sources
FSC® C008047
FSC
www.fsc.org

PAGE 4
FLOWERS, BOOK AND FRUIT ON ROUND TABLE, 1961
Oil on board, 91.5 x 61cm (36 x 24in). The Estate of Cyril Mann / courtesy of Piano Nobile,
Robert Travers (Works of Art) Ltd

Cyril renders bold shadow effects as well as the movement of light emanating from the fruit
plate, books and flowers.

THE GIRL IN THE GREEN JUMPER

My Life with the Artist Cyril Mann

Renske Mann

INTRODUCTION BY MARK HUDSON

PIMPERNEL
PRESS LTD
www.pimpernelpress.com

CONTENTS

Introduction by Mark Hudson 6

INTRODUCTION

By Mark Hudson

When it comes to deciding the most tragic British artist of the twentieth century, Cyril Mann must be a contender. Possessed of formidable gifts as a painter, Mann made a number of genuinely innovative breakthroughs over the course of a near sixty-year career, and certainly had the potential to become one of the most important figurative painters of his time. Yet beset by very severe mental problems – bipolar disorder probable Asperger's syndrome, not to mention a chip on his shoulder the size of a house – Mann had an apparently unerring instinct for turning each moment of promise into bitter disappointment.

His irascibility and paranoid belligerence alienated friends and powerful potential supporters, not to mention his two wives and his own daughter, as he fought his way from one catastrophic breakdown to another. He succumbed to a heart attack in the midst of a final devastating mental collapse, dying aged sixty-eight in 1980.

Where some great artists have been able to turn the most calamitous personal circumstances into the stuff of posthumous romantic myth – think of Amadeo Modigliani, Arshile Gorky or John Minton – Cyril Mann has remained a pitifully obscure figure. Bellicose and opinionated, he refused to align himself with any influential movements or groupings of artists, and failed even to benefit from the twentieth-century fascination with artistic derangement, because his work itself is nothing if not lucid.

Such is the figure described in John Russell Taylor's excellent monograph *The Sun is God: The Life and Work of Cyril Mann* (Lund Humphries, 1999), an artist who was very much his own worst enemy, who was almost literally unbearable, even, you feel, to himself.

SELF-PORTRAIT WITH A CIGARETTE, c.1952
Oil on canvas, 33 x 25cm (13 x 10in), Private Collection

This self-portrait gives a good impression of how Cyril looked when we first met. He's a serious, middle-aged man with a balding dome of a forehead and a grim, determined expression. A cigarette dangles from his mouth, ash perilously close to falling off. He renders every line and wrinkle on his ageing face with pitiless honesty. His hair – once, he told me, like a lion's mane – is rapidly receding and far too long for respectability. Cyril's violet-blue, sunken eyes mirror his physical and mental suffering, as I learned later.

If this poignant and revealing memoir by Mann's second wife, Renske van Slooten, does nothing to contradict the essentials of this view, it adds vital new dimensions to our understanding of Mann, both as artist and human being. The result is a far more rounded, sympathetic and engaging figure. The Mann revealed in these pages is still an enormously difficult, at times monstrous character, but he has too – on a good day – warmth, humour, emotional generosity and a total dedication to his art.

The Girl in the Green Jumper tells the story of how Renske, a twenty-year-old newly arrived from Holland in bleak, austerity-era London, meets Mann, then forty-eight, practically by chance, at an evening class in a dilapidated further education institute in Holborn in 1959. She falls in love with him, moves in with him, shares his poverty-stricken existence and becomes his model, muse and his greatest supporter over the twenty years until his death.

The result is a tragicomic and admirably frank and uncomfortable account of a May–December relationship, starting in a badly heated, post-war tower block, in which Renske's devotion to her 'British Van Gogh' only wavers in the final harrowing chapters.

The mystery of why a beautiful, energetic and enterprising young woman should have hitched her colours to an impecunious, profoundly troubled and – judging by all available pictures – far from beautiful man twenty-eight years her senior is one of the factors that keeps you reading this intriguing memoir. That Renske's passion feels credible, if not always easily comprehensible, is a testament to her determination to stick to a course of action once she's embarked on it.

She can see the genius in Cyril's light-filled interiors and hallucinatory streetscapes, and nothing – neither the near total indifference of the art market nor the often spectacular perversity of her artist-lover himself – will stop her sharing that perception with the rest of the world, by tirelessly writing letters, organizing exhibitions and exploiting every possible contact that comes her way.

More than that, however, Cyril himself – utterly impossible though he may be on many levels – brings to these pages a certain hang-dog charisma, a primal life-force, considerable humour and, most importantly, a sense of total integrity concerning his art. For Mann, art isn't merely a vehicle for his vanities and manias, still less a means of making money, but the moral stuff of life, whose inalienable values must never be compromised, and of which, we are persuaded, he has a profound understanding.

Renske drinks deep from the well of knowledge of a man who is – despite the faults that leave even his elder daughter hating him at times – we are made to feel, not only admirable, but in many respects likeable, even loveable; which isn't quite the same as saying we'd like to have spent a great deal of time with Cyril Mann.

The narrative's other great driver is the certainty – felt practically from the first sentence – that the whole thing will end extremely badly, and our curiosity to see how this will be played out. Without giving too much away, Renske details her changing attitudes towards her husband with disarming honesty. If her sense of regret that she wasn't able to fully stay the course and save Mann from himself feels only decent, it's fair to say that most of us couldn't have tolerated a week, never mind twenty years, of Cyril's volcanic mood swings.

An incidental pleasure, particularly in the book's early stages, is its evocation of an ill-heated, ill-fed, still bomb-ravaged post-war London. Through this grim and battered metropolis, which is seen in some of Mann's best paintings, we can feel the imminent upsurge of the 1960s and social and cultural developments of which Cyril seems barely aware, except as an irritating distraction, but which Renske longs to embrace in the form of Beatles records and white Courrèges boots, as her career in PR takes off.

You may find yourself wondering at moments whose story you're reading. Is this first and foremost a book about Cyril Mann told from the point of view of his second wife and greatest supporter? Or is it essentially Renske's autobiography, in which Cyril plays an undeniably important role?

The answer comes in the book's closing sentences, when she reaffirms her pledge, made in the first days of her relationship with Mann, that she will do everything in her power to promote him and his work.

After all the many exhibitions that Renske has organized behind the scenes, the many pieces of writing she has commissioned on the subject of her late husband's work, over a period of sixty years, this book gives an unflinching account of the tragic background to these endeavours – and to an extraordinary creative partnership. You're left feeling that Renske's efforts have been not only morally, but artistically, entirely justified.

Mark Hudson
Author and art critic

e. Mann. 56

Chapter 1

MEETING CYRIL

My first glimpse of Cyril Mann was through the door of a classroom in Kingsway Day College, a further education institute in Holborn, London. As I stood on tiptoe peering through the window, I could see Cyril with his back to me, slumped at his desk in front of his students with their easels and drawing boards. His hair, what there was of it, was long and unkempt. He wore a crumpled tweed jacket with leather elbow patches. He wasn't tall, a bit over five foot at most. To me, barely out of my teens and recently arrived from Holland, he looked old, at least fifty. Yet before I'd even seen his face, I felt drawn to him.

He seemed not to notice as I slipped into the room and took a place at the back. It was the last evening class of term, a week before Christmas in 1959. Cyril looked half asleep and exhausted. His whole air was scruffy, neglected and unloved. Yet it was easy to see from their silence and concentration that his students revered him.

I knew nothing about this man and hadn't seen any of his paintings. He barely looked at me when we were introduced. I strained to hear what he was saying in a soft gruff voice. 'What's your name, chooky?' he asked absently in what I later realized was a Midlands accent. 'Renske, Mr Mann,' I replied. 'Fine, Ronsk, we're finished in a few minutes.'

He was unlike any man I had ever met. Deep-set, downturned eyes gave him a sad look. I noticed his florid complexion, his sunken cheeks and sensitive mouth. His air of distracted intensity reminded me of a sketch I had seen of Leonardo da Vinci in old age.

My middle-class Dutch family and boyfriends had warned me that Englishmen were arrogant and often effeminate. I imagined a future English boyfriend or husband looking like the actor David Niven, wearing a formal pin-stripe suit, with bowler and cane. In his suede shoes, considered rather disreputable in those days, there was nothing formal about Cyril.

SELF-PORTRAIT, 1956

Conté crayon and chalks, 54 x 37cm (21 x 14½in), National Portrait Gallery, London

Every hair, an affair, Cyril joked. In truth, he fretted about his balding pate: would it put off women? He needn't have worried. After his first wife, Mary, abandoned him, taking their daughter, Sylvia, there was a string of affairs and girlfriends. I too fell for him at first sight, despite being twenty-eight years his junior.

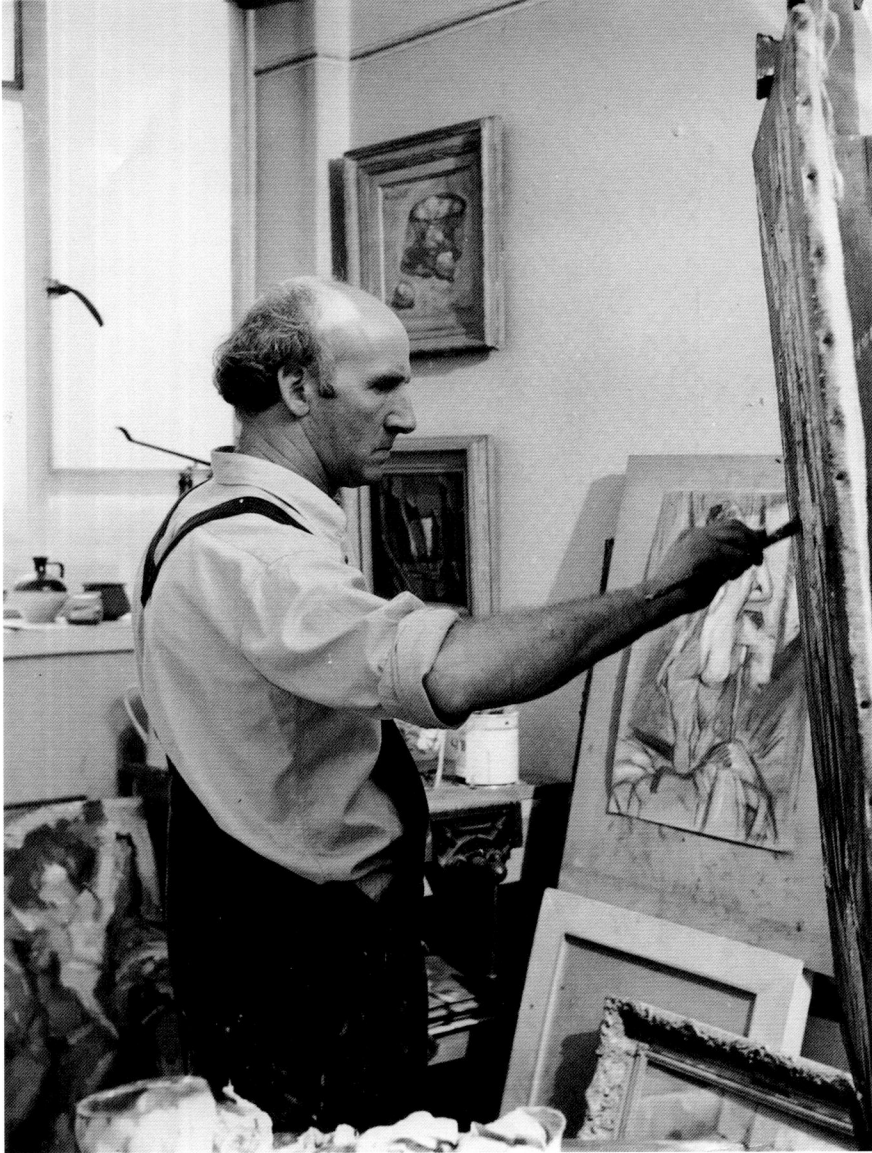

ABOVE Cyril was clean-shaven when we met in 1959. Jimmy Porteous, who took this picture of Cyril in his Bevin Court paint room, was the lead nurse at the Royal Free Hospital psychiatric unit. Jimmy had played a part in sectioning him during his serious nervous breakdown and locked him in a padded cell. They became friends for life.

OPPOSITE Cyril and me with one of his paintings, taken by Odham Press journalist Eric Sykes, in 1962.

How do you explain charisma? Even though he was a mystery to me, it seemed to me at the time Cyril had it in spades. As he moved among the students, I could sense his mental and physical suffering, his boredom and frustration at this demanding job, which kept him from what he loved most: painting. Working intently on a picture beside me was an exceptionally handsome student, a guy called Vic. He was my own age and gorgeous, but I only had eyes for Cyril.

At the end of the class, we all went for a coffee at the Kardomah Coffee House in Kingsway. As I talked to Mr Mann — as I still thought of him — we discovered we lived on the same bus route. The No. 19 would take him to his flat near The Angel, Islington, and me back to my Highbury Grove hostel. Had we not gone on that bus together, we might never have met again.

Hoping to smoke at least two cigarettes before he got off at The Angel, Mr Mann and I clambered to the top of the bus. It was quiet and late evening when Cyril said, 'You're a dangerous woman to know for a man of my age.' What could he possibly mean? How could I be dangerous to anyone?

Greatly daring, I ventured, 'Mr Mann, would you show me your pictures one day?'

'Yes,' he replied. 'I'd love to take you upstairs and show you my etchings.' I was puzzled. My schoolgirl English didn't extend to double entendres. He noticed my baffled expression, adding: 'We could meet tomorrow. I'll pick you up outside the cinema at The Angel, next to Lyons.'

ABOVE My glamorous parents: Maximiliaan van Slooten and his Dutch-Indonesian bride, Nini, on their wedding day, 24 June 1937, in Bandung, Indonesia.

OPPOSITE Me in 1965, in my mid-twenties and, said Cyril, looking like a Vermeer milkmaid.

Chapter 2

ABOUT ME

I had arrived in London from Holland the previous July, a month before I turned twenty, with £20 in my pocket as a leaving gift from my parents. I had a job lined up as a bilingual Dutch-English secretary for a Dutch company in the City. I stayed at the Young Women's Christian Association hostel in Highbury, North London, sharing a dormitory with four other girls of my own age.

The job paid £9 a week with £3 deducted for tax and insurance. With luncheon vouchers and other meals provided at the YWCA, I could manage easily. I found London exciting after the repressive atmosphere of my hometown, Dordrecht. On TV a boy called Cliff Richard sang: 'Got myself a crying, sleeping, walking, talking, living doll.' Marty Wilde and Tommy Steele were stirring Britain's youth on the rapidly developing pop scene.

Yet while I was utterly alone in this strange and frightening new city, I wasn't quite the innocent abroad my looks and heavily accented English might suggest. I had already escaped a doomed love affair with a married man fourteen years my senior. Born before the Second World War, my childhood had been unhappy and my education truncated.

Although my name is Dutch, I'm of mixed race, born in 1939 into a well-off Dutch-Indonesian family in what was then the Dutch East Indies. My family lived in the university town of Bandung, Java, where my Jewish-Dutch father, Maximiliaan van Slooten, was a civil engineer and my Dutch-Indonesian mother, Nini, had been a newspaper journalist before they married.

The Japanese invasion of Java in 1942 brought my parents' opulent lifestyle to an abrupt end. At the time, my father was doing military service as an officer. He was

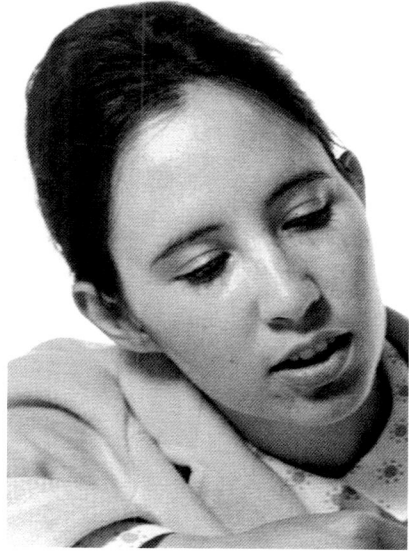

Life was easy and full of promise for wealthy colonials like my family in the Dutch East Indies before the war. My brother, Bastiaan (1938–2011) – eleven months older than me – and I grew up in a beautiful house with servants and luxury cars. When the Japanese invaded Java in 1943, that idyllic lifestyle came to an end.

taken prisoner of war, forced to labour on the notorious Burma railway. For three years he was missing. We didn't know if he was dead or alive.

When the Japanese army requisitioned our house, my mother with her two small children moved with other female family members into my grandmother's house in Bandung. There we spent the rest of the war years.

Being of mixed race, we were lucky: unlike the pure Dutch, we were not rounded up and interned in prison camps. Indonesians collaborated with the Japanese and we were not seen as enemies. In Burma, my father's officer status and university degree earned him the respect of his captors, probably saving his life in the jungle.

Native Indonesians collaborated with the Japanese as they had hoped to achieve independence from the hated Dutch. They had not reckoned on Japan losing the war.

When my father returned from Burma after the war, he was so exhausted, sick and emaciated that we didn't recognize him. He was devastated to see the children he had left behind malnourished and suffering from beriberi, the nutritional disorder with various symptoms including swollen bellies.

Me and my big brother, aged two and three respectively, in our birth place, Bandung, Indonesia, before the Japanese invasion.

My parents moved from Bandung to Batavia, known today as Jakarta. Their hopes for a fresh start were soon dashed. In 1949, guerilla warfare broke out as the Indonesians revived their struggle for independence. Under international pressure following India's independence from Britain, the Dutch government finally ceded control of their colony.

Dr Sukarno, Indonesia's first president, issued an ultimatum to Dutch-Indonesians: if you want to stay, give up your Dutch passports. If not, you leave with nothing. My parents could have stayed but would not agree to relinquish their Dutch nationality. Along with hundreds of thousands of others, we were banished at short notice with only a suitcase to our name.

Before leaving Batavia, my father made a last-ditch attempt to persuade the president, Dr Sukarno, to let us take a few possessions to the Netherlands. My father owned two oil paintings by a celebrated Indonesian artist, Affandi, which he planned to present as a gift to the president for his art collection. Before the war my father and the president had both graduated in engineering from Bandung University and he hoped that as he was known to admire Affandi, Sukarno would respond to his generosity.

My father had bought the large Expressionist paintings two years earlier, hanging them side by side on our wall. One depicted a preening cockerel. The other was a still life of red canna flowers. Aged eight, it was the first time I became aware of art, not of the pretty, photographic type, but bold, colourful and expressive images. I loved the canna still life but loathed the cockerel painting. It reminded me of a cockfight my father had once taken me to see.

A mob of Indonesians, sitting on their haunches and smoking kreteks – foul-smelling roll-ups – were stroking a magnificent, plumed creature with razor blades attached to its feet. Its cockerel opponent was restrained nearby by other men. 'It is nowhere near as strong,' my father predicted while placing his bets. It would soon be torn to shreds in the fight to the death, he laughed.

I barely dared look, nauseated by heat, noise and cigarette smoke. I climbed back in my father's jeep, disgusted but desperately concealing my anguish and terror. Children were seen, but were definitely not meant to be heard.

My father hoped against hope that he could strike a friendship deal with Sukarno. In common with all Indonesians, the president had no first name. He was popularly known as Bung, or Brother: Bung Karno for short. One day our two Affandi paintings disappeared from the wall. A limousine arrived to take my father to the president.

Apparently, the meeting was affable. Sukarno was pleased to accept my father's paintings but there the friendship ended. No exception could be made. We left the land of our birth a few months later deprived of anything of real value.

Years earlier my father had befriended a Chinese builder. They had decided to go into business together as property developers. My father fancied himself as an architect. He was qualified to make all the calculations for complex building design. Working every weekend with his Chinese business partner – who provided the finance – they proceeded to develop and build properties in a new post-war residential area in Batavia called Kebayoran.

On Sundays, it was my father's turn to look after my elder brother, Bas, and me. He took us on a long, dusty drive in his jeep, leaving us waiting, seemingly for hours, until he and his partner had finished their inspection rounds. Then the Chinese friend took us home for a family meal.

My father never had Indonesian friends whom he liked and respected as much as he did this business partner. We were invited to family weddings lasting for days. I remember the deafening noise, like strange caterwauling, of the Chinese music and opera.

When my father's friend heard that we were soon to be expelled with nothing, he wanted to help us. I'm not sure if money secretly changed hands between them, but I know he offered my father a gift. He promised to send two valuable, hand-knotted silk Chinese carpets to Holland, awaiting our arrival a few months later. We went to the factory where the carpets were being hand-knotted by girls barely older than myself. In line with his modern, Western taste, my father chose a warm pink-beige shade, plain and with just a small flower motif in one corner. He accepted his gift with gratitude.

My family arrived in Rotterdam as penniless refugees. Soon after, the Netherlands granted self-rule to its colony, the East Indies. The Dutch had been far from welcoming to their dark-skinned compatriots with funny accents. Before the war, my privileged family had been settled in Java for generations. They had intermarried whilst keeping a safe social distance from native Indonesians. We spoke their language, but few could speak ours.

It would be years before our Chinese carpets would see the light of day. In 1952, two years after our arrival in Holland, my parents finally moved into a new-built apartment on the outskirts of The Hague.

Hindsight is a fine thing: had my father managed to hang on to his Affandi paintings, they would have been worth a small fortune today . . . The Indonesian Expressionist artist's work is fetching huge sums, an oil painting selling for over $1 million at a recent New York auction.

Just as the refugee van Slooten family settled down in Dordrecht, Renske left her parents bewildered and upset when she married Cyril without their permission. Here is the family she left behind: Max and Nini van Slooten with Bastiaan, Adriaan and Francisca, born in 1950 and 1953 respectively.

Chapter 3

NOT WELCOME
IN OUR MOTHERLAND

In 1950 we sailed from Batavia's seaport, Tanjung Priok, in the *Sibajak*, a luxury liner turned troopship. My grandmother and I slept in bunks in the stifling bowels below deck. My mother had her own cabin. Eight months pregnant, she was badly seasick during the month-long crossing.

The *Sibajak* was stuffed to the gunnels with refugees. She refuelled in Colombo, then stopped at Port Said before sailing through the Suez Canal to Europe and arriving in the war-damaged port of Rotterdam.

My father had arranged emergency accommodation in a boarding house in The Hague. My brother Adrie was born on my eleventh birthday, barely a month after our arrival. The city was and remains a hub for Dutch-Indonesians, or Indos as we were known. For authentic Indonesian food, always eat in The Hague, not in Amsterdam.

My parents soon looked to escape from our boarding house. They found rooms behind a Spar grocery store owned by a young couple with several children. Two of their boys suffered from dwarfism and were barely taller than their baby sister. I quickly bonded with those little chaps, who treated me with respect. Dutch children at my primary school bullied and scared me.

I needed private lessons to catch up. I had missed vital education during and since the war. A Dutch teacher spoon-fed me through the equivalent of the British eleven-plus. I managed to scrape through and went to an all-girls grammar school. Then I disgraced myself and failed to keep up. I used to stare blankly at the blackboard and never did my homework. My father was teaching mathematics at that same school. I was a dunce, his colleagues told him. My self-confidence plummeted. I was miserable.

When I was thirteen, my grandmother died suddenly. I saw her body in an open coffin and was petrified, screaming in terror.

My mother had never visited Holland before. She couldn't cook and knew nothing about housekeeping. Meanwhile, my father's Bandung University degree was no longer recognized, which was a massive setback. His only option was to study for a second Civil Engineering degree, this time at Delft University. Needs must – he was still only in his forties and needed a job. As he was exceptionally brainy, he qualified in record time.

After five years of German occupation, the Netherlands was far from prosperous. Afflicted by massive food and housing shortages, the Dutch dreaded the sudden influx of 300,000 dark-skinned penniless refugees. Our situation was like that of the Ugandan Asians who were similarly expelled by the African dictator, Idi Amin.

I was shocked by narrow-minded racism. My handsome elder brother, Bas, was rejected by a girlfriend's parents because he was a 'peanut', the slang used to denigrate our mixed-racial heritage. Why peanut? Because it is light brown and used in Indonesian cooking. Holland may have a reputation for liberalism, but not so in provincial Dordrecht when I lived there.

My father was appointed lecturer in mechanical engineering at the local technical college. My sister, Francisca, was born in 1953. My wealthy Jewish grandmother had left my parents a useful legacy. A successful businesswoman, she had foreseen problems and had been the only family member to salt away her investments and savings before the war. My parents had invested my grandmother's legacy in a spacious semi-detached house, designed by my father, in an upmarket, leafy area overlooking a marina.

For the first time, I went to a mixed school. Life was looking up: I made friends and did surprisingly well, passing O-level equivalents in maths and four languages with good grades. I longed to go to art school, but my parents decided otherwise. At sixteen I did what girls were expected to do and learned shorthand typing. Then I had to get a job.

It was freezing in winter. My bicycle was my only form of transport, rain or shine. In the typing pool of a chemical factory along with other girls, I rhythmically typed the same letter fifty times a day. Except for names and addresses, each letter was identical. Photocopiers and word processors had not been invented. Three errors and we had to retype from scratch. If we failed to reach our quota, we were threatened with the sack.

The office manager hovered around, ensuring nobody chatted or wasted time in the loo. Our working day started 8.30 a.m., ending nine hours later with thirty minutes for lunch. We worked half days on Saturdays. I was scared of the office manager but even more so of my parents. Had I been sacked my strict mother would have made my life hell. Children never answered back those days.

For lunch I took white-bread sandwiches slathered in margarine and sprinkled with sugar. My poor teeth suffered horribly. My parents pocketed half my pay. I was hard-up and resentful. At sixteen I already smoked and cigarettes were expensive. It was hard for my parents with four children to make ends meet. A contribution from grown-up children was expected.

I hated Dordrecht and couldn't wait to leave. When I arrived in London in July 1959, I was still a teenager, turning twenty a month later.

Cyril and Renske on a family visit to Dordrecht, with her mother, Nini van Slooten (left), and an aunt and uncle.

Qualified in Dutch, English and French shorthand, I had landed a proper secretarial job with a work permit. I was proud of my knowledge of languages. Colleagues laughed when I told them that my boss had given me a French letter. Britain was much wealthier than the Netherlands. I was earning four times as much in London as I had been in Dordrecht: £9 a week, instead £9 per month.

I loved the companionship and communal living with other girls in the YWCA hostel. Freedom at last! Despite a strict ban on male visitors supervision was minimal. The dilapidated converted Victorian edifice could have been a stage set for a creepy Hitchcock movie. Nobody cared how it looked, inside or out.

It was midsummer. We relaxed in the large back garden, chatting till nightfall, a small United Nations group of girls from all over the world, attracted to London like moths to a flame. Our tall, rickety windows overlooked Highbury Grove, Islington, where red double-decker buses would whisk us in a few short stops to the Centre of the World: magnificent Piccadilly Circus, with its huge neon advertising displays, the likes of which I had never seen before.

The bedrooms on several floors could each accommodate up to five beds. I never asked how many girls were staying at a time. From the queue in the dining room, I guessed more than fifty. We ate pallid meals, cabbage cooked to death, greasy chops, but we didn't care. Virtually everyone smoked.

Some girls were college students, others were on long-term holidays. A few slaved away in Foyles, then famous as the world's biggest bookshop. Somehow, Foyles could arrange a temporary student work permit. It paid a pittance, but most girls preferred working as sales assistants to being an au pair.

One woman, Madihah from Jordan, was in her late twenties, slightly older than most of us. She had achieved a big step on the career ladder, working as a reporter for the BBC World Service in the Arabic section at Bush House. Madihah commissioned me on behalf of the BBC to write an article on Dutch historical marriage customs. My first-ever paid writing assignment earned me the princely sum of four guineas.

Madihah translated my feature into Arabic and I read it phonetically during her broadcast on women's issues. Such an opportunity could never have happened in Dordrecht, I bragged in a letter to my parents.

Our communal living room centred around a small black-and-white TV set. With just two channels, the BBC (later BBC1) and a commercial channel with paid-for advertising, there were never arguments about what to watch. When BBC2 was launched in the early 1960s, most families didn't bother to buy a new aerial. This prevented reception of slightly more highbrow programmes broadcast by the new channel.

In our hostel, we were not interested in highbrow – *Sunday Night at the Palladium* was our favourite. Our small set would be on maximum volume so we could sing along with our teen idols. Tommy Steele, whose movie *Tommy the Toreador* had just come out, was one. We lusted after handsome Marty Wilde and swooned at the sight of drop-dead gorgeous Cliff Richard.

Before long, friends couldn't resist trying to matchmake and pair me off with a brother or cousin. I met some highly educated Greek-Cypriot boys. They were university students, impeccably polite and intelligent young men who had passed their A-levels the previous year.

I had arrived in London with a suitcase full of clothes made by my mother. She was a superb dressmaker. My skirts were knee-length – mini-skirts were still to come – worn over scratchy, bulky petticoats. My cinched, belted waist and flared hem created an elegant silhouette. I ruined my feet in stiletto heels – great for jiving but a nightmare for walking.

Madihah from Jordan introduced me to an eligible suitor, a rich, young businessman from Saudi Arabia who asked: 'Are you a virgin?' I told him it was none of his business.

I plastered my face with Max Factor Pancake, great for covering spots and freckles. Gaudy pink lipstick complemented my sophisticated new London look. In those pre-Vidal Sassoon days, my black hair was permed into short tight curls styled as a bob which needed professional shampoo-and-sets to prevent frizz. I could afford it on my generous weekly wage.

As summer turned into autumn, I bought an unsexy warm duffle coat with leather toggle fastening. I wore it when I first met Cyril the week before Christmas. No wonder he barely noticed me!

It was not always peace and tranquility in our hostel. Ugly clashes arose among some girls. Personality, prejudice and politics were usually to blame.

Madihah disliked my friendship with a Jewish Dutch girl newly arrived from Amsterdam. As a radio journalist, she recalled the 1948 partition of Palestine and Israel, blaming its subsequent traumas on Jews.

My new Jewish friend could barely hide her dislike of a beautiful German girl who shared our room. During the war she had been passed around and kept hidden by Dutch families. It had saved her life, but her young mother perished in a concentration camp.

I learned later that the Netherlands had the greatest number of Jewish victims in Western Europe. According to the Anne Frank Organization, hundreds of thousands of Jews were betrayed by their fellow Dutch citizens, who were rewarded with bounty payments by the occupying Gestapo.

While living in the YWCA hostel, a Cypriot boy, Criton Tomazos, took me dancing at the 100 Club in Oxford Street and at Hammersmith Palais in West London. Studying to be an architect, he said one day: 'I know you like art. You should meet my old teacher.' Which is how I came to find myself looking through the doorway of Cyril Mann's evening class, and – less than twenty-four hours later – standing outside Lyons self-service restaurant at The Angel, Islington, waiting for him.

ST PAUL'S FROM BANKSIDE, *c*.1952
Oil on board, 46 x 56cm (18¼ x 22in), Private Collection

One painting that immediately caught my attention showed the dome of St Paul's looming over the rooftops from across the Thames, painted in the early 1950s, from the exact spot where the Millennium Bridge spans the river beside Tate Modern today. At first the picture appeared almost monochrome. As I went on looking at it, I saw that the greys were shot through with blue and yellow and warm pink. The tiniest highlights of shifting sunlight picked out a distant church tower. To see London properly, Cyril said, the city should be viewed on a grey day. 'One day people will recognize my qualities as an artist purely on the strength of my ability to perceive greys in their infinite variety,' he said.

Chapter 4

OUR FIRST DATE

Excited at the prospect of spending time with a real artist, I had arrived early, wearing a brand-new pair of red stilettos that were already killing me. I waited and waited, but Mr Mann didn't appear. After half an hour I decided to give it another five minutes before leaving. Then I gave it another five minutes, and another and another. Had I decided to head back to the hostel at that moment, the entire course of my life – and Cyril's too – would have been different.

He arrived, hurrying along the pavement, confessing he had fallen asleep while reading a book. When he awoke, he'd rushed out, but he assumed I'd have long since gone, as any sensible girl would have done.

The first thing Cyril said was that he liked my red shoes. Later I discovered why. He had recently been dumped by his girlfriend, who had also worn red shoes when they first met. For now, I was utterly absorbed in the moment. He suggested we head back to his place to look at his paintings.

Cyril's flat was on the top floor of a high-rise council block, Bevin Court in Islington, an inner London borough. It had magnificent views and was crammed with books, sculptures, pictures and battered old furniture. On that first visit I was too focused on Cyril – and his paintings – really to notice my surroundings. His pictures were mostly small, rather dark and gloomy. They were among the most beautiful I'd ever seen, depicting London streets and bomb sites, which he had painted directly facing the sun. The light seemed to flash and shatter against the city's blackened walls and broken ground.

I knew little about art. I'd visited the Tate Gallery where I had seen Turner's paintings. I sensed that there was a 'family resemblance' between the great Turner and Cyril's paintings. He explained that Turner was one of his great heroes. 'He was working class like me,' he said with pride. 'He was greater, more revolutionary and more original than any French Impressionist. But Brits are not as clever as the French or Americans at promoting artists. That's why Turner is relatively unknown abroad. The Louvre only owns a couple of his paintings.' My art education had begun.

Then he turned to me and said, 'I'd love to paint you. Would you pose for me?' I was astonished and flattered that such a wonderful artist might think I'd make a good model. Yes, of course, I replied. I promised to come back to his tiny, cluttered flat after Christmas.

ABOVE DARK SATANIC MILLS, 1925
Oil on canvas, 48 x 54.5cm (19 x 21½in), Private Collection

This is the earliest painting still extant, done by Cyril aged only 14. He was considered a child prodigy, the youngest boy at the time ever to have won a scholarship to study painting at the Nottingham School of Art.

OPPOSITE Cyril as a boy, taken in Nottingham just before he left for Canada in 1925.

Chapter 5

ABOUT CYRIL

I'd never heard of Cyril before that fateful visit to his evening class, which was hardly surprising. Despite well-received exhibitions, his name would have meant little even to regular habitués of the London art scene. From childhood, Cyril had hit peaks of brilliance and attracted attention in ways that seemed to presage future greatness. Yet his life was marked by tragedy from the start.

His father, William Alloysius, spent much of his life in an asylum, having suffered shell shock in the First World War. Both his elder and younger brothers, Will and Austin, had died in tragic accidents. Will was crushed by a lift in Nottingham's Midland Hotel, where he worked in the 1920s. A decade later, Austin drowned in the River Trent while his wife and children picnicked on the riverbank.

Cyril was the youngest student ever to enrol in the prestigious Nottingham School of Art. He was awarded a scholarship aged twelve, needing special dispensation to leave normal schooling. Already his prodigious painting skills are evident in his earliest picture still extant. *Dark Satanic Mills* is an extraordinary masterpiece from a boy then only fourteen. Yet, while his mother – Gertrude Nellie, known as Gertie, a tough, domineering working-class woman – harboured great hopes for her son, she forced him to leave art school at fifteen. His financial contribution was needed to help support the family. With his father permanently sectioned in the asylum, Gertie had to raise their four children alone, the family subsisting on a small war pension.

After leaving art school and working in an ill-paid clerical job, Cyril was desperate to escape. He headed to Canada as a trainee missionary aged fifteen, apprenticed to a local priest who saw great potential in him. He was expected to enter the priesthood, but amid the spectacular landscapes of British Columbia he began painting again. Soon he dropped all thoughts of religion. On the advice of the Canadian post-Impressionist Arthur Lismer – a Sheffield-born member of the now

PLACE DE LA CONCORDE, PARIS, 1937
Oil on canvas, 48 x 58cm (18³/₄ x 22³/₄in),
Private Collection

Cyril observes people silhouetted
against a fountain. He paints facing the
sun and is overjoyed. Pre-war Paris has,
at last, given him the creative freedom
denied to him as a student at the Royal
Academy Schools in London.

NOTTINGHAM HOUSES, *c.*1936

Oil on canvas, 61 x 51cm (24 x 20in), Private Collection

Cyril captures his mother, Gertie, as she is weeding her garden. His love of sunlight is already evident in this early painting.

AGAINST THE SUN, CANADA, *c.*1929
Oil on board, 19 x 24cm (7½ x 9½in), The Estate of Cyril Mann / courtesy of Piano Nobile,
Robert Travers (Works of Art) Ltd

Cyril is thought to be the only British artist to have been directly influenced by the now
famous Canadian Group of Seven landscape painters, one of whose members – Sheffield-born
Arthur Lismer – advised the young man to return to London for his art education.

PONT NEUF, PARIS, 1937
Oil on canvas, 38 x 46cm (15 x 18¼in), Collection Renske Mann

Cyril breathed a sigh of relief when he swapped the discipline of London's Royal Academy Schools for bohemian Paris where he could paint what he liked. For two years until the outbreak of war in 1939, he remained financially supported through a trust fund set up by his first sponsor, Erica Marx. Here are two of his earliest paintings. Cyril considered the romantic oil he painted of the Pont Neuf as his first masterpiece. The bridge is seen against the sun as fishermen cast off on its banks.

MY EARLIEST SELF-PORTRAIT, 1937

Oil on canvas, 28 x 22cm (11 x 8½in) Collection Renske Mann

An inscription on the back of the painting, done aged twenty-six, confirms that it is his earliest self-portrait.

ABOVE **THE RED LETTER BOX**, *c.*1949
Oil on canvas, 51 x 41cm (20 x 16in), The Estate of Cyril Mann / courtesy of Piano Nobile,
Robert Travers (Works of Art) Ltd
Cyril stares against the sun, partially obstructed by trees. Dazzling light splashes
around his feet. A passer-by in a blue coat faraway catches our eye against the darkly
silhouetted buildings.

OPPOSITE Cyril on leave from the army, photographed in 1941 with his first wife,
Mary Jervis-Read, and their toddler daughter, Sylvia, who grew up to be a published
author, poet and playwright.

famous Group of Seven – Cyril returned to Britain after six years determined to resume his artistic studies.

Cyril almost starved on the streets of Depression-era London, before he was taken up by a friend – the left-wing priest Oliver Fielding Clark – who persuaded the philanthropist Erica Marx to set up a trust fund for Cyril. It paid for his study at the Royal Academy Schools. Her generous sponsorship continued when he abandoned the discipline of his alma mater to further his art education in Paris under the Scottish Colourist J. D. Fergusson. There he met his first wife, Mary Jervis-Read. Soon after marrying, the outbreak of the Second World War forced the couple to rush back to England. Mary was expecting a baby.

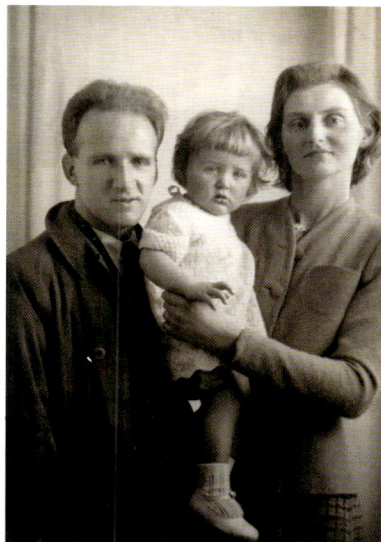

Conscripted and serving as a gunner for six years during the war, Cyril resented never being invited to be an official war artist. He blamed it on his working-class roots, but his daughter, Sylvia, thought otherwise. She suspected that her father's temperament was considered unstable by his superiors. He never got on with his superior officers, nor did he bond with men in lower ranks. He loathed communal living. The war, he said, was six wasted years when he produced virtually no art.

Demobbed in 1946, he returned to Mary and little Sylvia. They desperately looked for jobs and housing in Shoreditch, a badly damaged inner London borough. Surrounded by bomb sites, Cyril began painting looking directly into the sun and creating apocalyptic visions of the stricken city.

Life was an immense struggle for the young couple, but hopes were raised when Cyril's paintings were included in an important exhibition at one of the world's largest private art galleries, Wildenstein's in Bond Street. When the great Dutch-French Fauve painter Kees van Dongen saw these paintings at the 'Artists of Fame and Promise' exhibition in 1948, he declared them the only works there that would endure into posterity. But with war just over, the public was weary of destruction: Cyril's paintings didn't sell well. He went on exhibiting throughout the 1950s, but every new sign of hope was almost inevitably followed by crushing disappointment.

SUNLIT NUDE WITH BLUE DRESSING GOWN, 1963
Oil on canvas, 52 x 76cm (20½ x 30in), The Estate of Cyril Mann / courtesy of Piano Nobile, Robert Travers (Works of Art) Ltd

Despite communal central heating, our flat in Bevin Court was freezing. I remember lying on a green Indian bedspread, I wanted to doze off. Cyril wrapped a blue dressing gown around my hips to keep me warm. I shut my eyes against the dazzle. He paints direct, without sketching first. 'It's taken me thirty years to learn how to do this,' he growls. The sun speeds through our window, casting shadows against the wall. He howls with frustration when I move an inch. He's drenched in sweat at the strain. This is not how I imagined art.

Chapter 6

THE ARTIST'S MODEL

I had no idea what hard work modelling would be. It was always cold in Cyril's flat, with just one small radiator well away from the bed. Even the most comfortable pose soon became hell. Cyril painted quickly, but once he'd got started he was reluctant to let me rest, and he wouldn't allow me to read or listen to music. He, on the other hand, was in heaven: he had found a young woman prepared to pose for him at no cost, quietly and without distraction.

When I first got undressed to pose nude for him, he looked me up and down with a critical eye. 'Perfect breasts,' he observed. 'Not too big, not too small. You can thank your Indonesian forebears for those.' We'd known each other for about a month, and already we were perfectly at ease with each other, as if we'd known each other all our lives.

Those were the most comforting words anyone had ever said to me about my Dutch-Indonesian ancestry. Back in Holland, the darker-skinned immigrants among us were subject to outright racial abuse. I was self-conscious about the Asian cast of my features, though our family fared better than most as we were light-skinned.

'Dutch people aren't pretty,' Cyril observed. 'They are big and coarse-looking. The Indonesian influx will improve and refine their features in future generations.' No one had ever said anything so flattering about my mixed-racial background. Cyril wasn't out to flatter. His was a statement of fact. It made me love him all the more.

He went on to paint many nudes of me. One really stuck in my mind. My dressing gown was wrapped around my hips and legs, providing a splash of colour and keeping my feet warm, as I lay motionless for hours on our pale green cotton bedspread. Sunlight streamed through our steel-framed Crittall windows on to my breasts, arms and shoulders, light seeming to explode off my body in all directions.

STUDIO CORNER, 1961

Oil on canvas, 86 x 76cm (33³/₄ x 30in), The Estate of Cyril Mann / courtesy of Piano Nobile, Robert Travers (Works of Art) Ltd

Our bedroom is out of bounds. That's where Cyril stores hundreds of unsold paintings, stacked against the wall. A large mahogany chest is full to overflowing. An open drawer reveals my blue dressing gown, contrasting with the many shades of brown. A large hog's-hair brush lies on top of the wooden stool.

Chapter 7

MOVING IN

By February 1960, I had been in London for six months. My job with the Dutch company was fine for the moment, but I was bored with the communal hostel lifestyle. I needed some independence. Did Cyril know of anywhere else I could stay? Yes, he did. His former girlfriend, Alison Dale, lived in a flat just around the corner that had a spare bedroom. 'But I'd rather live here with you,' I blurted out.

This was easier said than done. Bevin Court, the high-rise block where Cyril lived, had only one small bedroom, used to store unsold paintings, easels and art objects. Cyril slept on a single bed in the living room where he did his painting and sculpture. 'We can easily share the bed,' I said. We were both small and didn't need much room. Cyril was only two inches taller than me, so I didn't see the single bed as a problem. I was passionately in love with him and didn't care if people couldn't understand why.

I gave in my notice at the YWCA and moved in with Cyril. My colleagues at the office were horrified. Here was I, a recent arrival in London, moving in with a much older man I hardly knew. It was considered scandalous then to live with somebody of the opposite sex unless you were married. People looked down on Cyril's council block. Living in social housing carried a stigma among the middle-class sections of society.

And there was another complication. Cyril was married. While he'd been separated from his wife, Mary, for many years, they had never bothered to divorce as neither intended to remarry. And Cyril's daughter, Sylvia, was only a year younger than me.

My colleagues at the Dutch-owned company where I worked had been friendly and welcoming until I let slip that Cyril was still married and lived in a council flat. My boss contacted the Dutch embassy and asked them to inform my parents that I was living in sin and in grave moral danger. I was summoned back to Holland and asked to explain myself. But my family had reckoned without my determination and love for Cyril.

I told them that if they ordered me to return to Dordrecht – which they could legally do as the age of majority was then twenty-one – I would wait until I came of age and marry Cyril without their permission. 'After that,' I said, 'I never want to see you again.'

My parents feared that I was being groomed by an older man: Cyril was a year older than my mother. But the truth was that I was the one doing all the running and had been ever since I first met Cyril. He was my lover, protector, teacher and surrogate father. My childhood was over. Ignoring all the naysayers, I moved in with him. Most of all, I wanted to marry him, but he would have to divorce Mary first.

HOMAGE TO TINTORETTO, 1971
Oil on canvas, 91.5 x 76cm (36 x 30in), Private Collection

After seeing the Scuola Grande di San Rocco in Venice, Cyril dedicated this large flower painting to Jacopo Tintoretto (1518–94) back in London. During our holiday in Venice, we took turns to sightsee and look after our toddler, Amanda. I stumbled on the Scuola first, urging Cyril to visit the next day. Tintoretto was a born rebel who, like him, had come from humble roots.

Chapter 8

A DAY AT THE MUSEUM

I was nervous when soon after we met Cyril first took me to the National Gallery. Would it blow my cover? Would he discover my ignorance about paintings?

We stopped at Vincent's *Sunflowers*. His eyes filled with tears. 'Imagine how insanely jealous Gauguin must have been when he first saw this painting,' said Cyril. 'Van Gogh painted it specially for him when he was living in the Yellow House in Arles, and hoping to set up an artists' community.'

'It's impossible today to grasp how revolutionary Vincent's pictures were then. He broke every rule of traditional painting, but after him art would never be the same again. We all owe a debt to his groundbreaking vision. If only I had the courage to paint as badly as that!'

'What do you mean?', I asked, surprised. 'At the Royal Academy Schools, I was drilled to paint like an Old Master,' Cyril grumbled. 'Everything was about technique. For three years, I drew plaster casts.'

'I chucked in my place and left for Paris, needing creative freedom. Ever since, I have tried to "unlearn" what they taught me at the RA. Technique has become too important in my art and that's not good,' he went on. 'It sapped my courage and dulled creativity. Lack of daring is holding me back,' he said angrily.

'Consider the power and emotional thrust of those sunflowers,' he continued, punching my arm. 'You don't know how to look at a painting, do you? Look up close first,' he commanded. 'So close that you can smell the picture and impasto. Now step back and see it from a distance to get the full perspective.'

Vincent's technique was crude by academic standards, but the end result transcended everything, according to Cyril. 'He was primarily a draughtsman, rather than a painter, filling in his outlines, sometimes using the back of his brush and slapping on paint, using his fingers if that's what he felt like. You can sense his excitement.'

'This is no painting of sunflowers, it is Vincent's mad expression of them. That's why he's known as the father of Expressionism.'

He paced back and forth, almost sniffing the picture in reverie. I was clearly in the way. 'Off you go,' he ordered. 'Why don't you walk around and come back when you've had enough? Then you can tell me which two paintings you liked best.' He had clearly noticed my limited attention span.

Meekly but excitedly, I went off on my own. Like a proverbial chicken-without-a-head, I glanced at everything crossing my path. What was I looking for? No idea! There were acres of gloomy paintings from different periods and countries. Religious subjects, portraits, landscapes – nothing 'spoke to me'.

Ah, the Dutch artists, at least these were familiar and I loved them: Rembrandt, Vermeer, Frans Hals and my favourite: Jan Steen's comically chaotic domestic scenes.

I was exhausted. After an hour, boredom had set in when my eyes fell on a huge mythological picture which took my breath away. Minutes later, I stumbled across another beauty that moved me for different reasons.

Time to report to Cyril. I found him, snorting, gesticulating and still staring at Vincent's sunflowers. He grabbed my arm, directing me to a Cezanne landscape this time. 'Here's another self-taught genius, Renske. Like Vincent, he changed the way we see nature.'

'Cezanne was regarded as the "Father of Cubism", because he saw everything in terms of a cylinder, sphere and cone. He was far more complex than the Impressionists, giving solidity and structure to their feathery brush strokes. He broke new ground in perspective and, with Vincent, led people to see in a radically different way.'

He turned to me: 'Have you seen anything you liked?' he asked, seemingly as an afterthought. 'Two paintings,' I replied. 'A huge one, called *The Death of Actaeon*, by a Venetian artist called Titian. The second one was a religious painting by a Florentine, Piero della Francesca, called *The Baptism of Christ*.'

He looked at me, surprised and with rekindled interest: 'Why the Titian?' he asked. 'It's because everything in that picture moves,' I answered, trying to explain myself adequately.

Cyril nodded approvingly. 'Don't let fools tell you that Titian left that painting unfinished. He left it exactly as he wanted it, blurred and impressionistic, because that's how he captured the sense of movement, which you spotted.'

'But why Piero's *Baptism*?' he asked. 'I loved that for the opposite reason: everything in it is still and perfectly balanced, like classical architecture,' I mumbled. 'Which picture did you like best?' Cyril prodded. 'I loved them both equally,' I answered.

'As a teacher, most students see Titian as a sensuous romantic, but Piero's classicism appeals to their sense of order. It's unusual to like both equally. Remember that great paintings must always be a fusion of hand, head and heart,' he concluded.

Five years later, in 1965, the National Gallery acquired Cezanne's *Les Grandes Baigneuses*, depicting male and female bathers rising from a woodland glade, resembling rocks integral to the landscape. The painting was ridiculed for its crudely drawn figures. The $1.4 million price created a furore.

Cyril disagreed. 'Worth every penny,' he insisted. 'The National can't lose with this masterpiece.'

Chapter 9

BEVIN COURT

Cyril's tiny flat was on the seventh floor of Bevin Court, a high-rise modernist block designed immediately after the war by the Tecton practice led by the Russian émigré architect Berthold Lubetkin and completed in 1954. The Constructivist staircase at the heart of the building, with walkways radiating from a central triangular column, has since been visited and admired by architectural historians and students from all over the world. But the thing that excited the building's first residents wasn't its structure or appearance, but its modern amenities: bathrooms, hot water day and night, and communal central heating – luxuries in early 1950s Britain, and all included in the subsidized weekly rent from Finsbury Borough Council.

Having moved from a dingy Victorian building near what is now the Barbican, Cyril felt he had it made. The block's hill top position gave him unimpeded daylight and a fabulous view over the rooftops of London. His previous residence had been on the upper floors of a gold-bullion storage facility, with every one of its windows blocked with metal bars for security. There, the interior was so gloomy, the lights had to be kept on throughout the day. It couldn't have been worse for a painter of sunlight like Cyril.

In the 1950s Bevin Court was one of the highest buildings in London. Our kitchen window overlooked the Courtauld Institute's Vernon Square campus, recently established in an old school.

VIEW FROM WINDOW, 1960
Oil on canvas, 53 x 73cm
(20³/₄ x 28³/₄in), The Estate of
Cyril Mann / courtesy of Piano
Nobile, Robert Travers
(Works of Art) Ltd

As Cyril opens the curtains,
the sun shines. He places a
pewter jug with tulips on the
windowsill against the light.
All of London is at our feet.
The buildings are jumbled
and silhouetted against the
polluted sky. I watch as he
paints rapidly, without first
sketching. As soon as his
divorce comes through,
we're getting married.

STILL LIFE WITH BOTTLES, *c.*1952–5
Oil on board, 41.6 x 33.3cm (16⅓ x 13in), Collection Renske Mann

From 1952 to 1955, Cyril briefly explored shadow formations created in the glare of an
electric light bulb. The barred windows in his flat deprived him of daylight. He had given up
painting sombre London bomb sites outdoors. Now he concentrated on everyday objects in
his kitchen, determined to paint the shape of shadows as no artist has done before or since.

KIPPERS ON A STRIPED TABLECLOTH, *c.*1952–5
Oil on board, 30.5 x 35.6cm (12 x 14in), The Estate of Cyril Mann / courtesy of Piano Nobile, Robert Travers (Works of Art) Ltd

Adapting to the dimness of his previous environment had led Cyril into one of his most distinctive phases, forcing him to concentrate on what he called 'the other side of light', the veil-like shadow formations cast by everyday objects such as bottles, vegetables, kippers, loaves or books. The mostly small pictures of what became known as his 'solid-shadow period', with their vivid colours and strong use of line, are widely considered among Cyril's most groundbreaking works. Their formalized designs anticipate by decades artists such as Patrick Caulfield and Michael Craig Martin.

The eminent dealer Erica Brausen – director of the Hanover Gallery in Mayfair who had previously 'discovered' Francis Bacon – was so impressed by these paintings, she offered Cyril a one-man show. It was not to be. There weren't enough of these little solid-shadow pictures to fill a whole exhibition, and Cyril stopped doing them when he

London Borough of Islington

CYRIL MANN
1911–1980

Painter and sculptor

Lived and worked here
1956–1964

Islington People's Plaque

moved into Bevin Court in 1956 (after Mary had already walked out on him, taking their daughter Sylvia with her). This 'lost' exhibition was one of many disappointments that dogged Cyril's life, but he was so excited about the possibilities of his new, bright flat that he barely paused to think about it.

The quality of the daylight streaming through the large windows reawakened his obsession with painting sunlight, and how it affects and transforms everyday objects. His objective – in common with many great artists of the past – was to create a new, more vibrant realism. He wanted to make people see light and shadow in a new way. For him, light equalled movement that both fractured and enhanced the appearance of objects.

When I joined Cyril in Bevin Court, he said he was now ready to synthesize his theories on light and shadow into a new form of painting. He had been painting and experimenting for a quarter of a century, but from the 1960s onwards, there's a sense of total release in his work. His nudes – mostly of me – as well as his still life and flower paintings dating from this period are bold and free, with a euphoric, sensuous feeling for paint.

One day Cyril woke up, drew back the curtains and yelled at me, 'Don't move. Don't you fucking move!' The dazzling sunlight hit my torso as I stretched, with my body casting a shadow on the wall behind. Sunlight fell on the red cushion on the bed. Cyril said: 'You're a modern Venus. Not rising from a seashell, but from sheets and blankets. I must paint this now!' Within minutes, he had dragged in his easel, palette and tins of paint.

It was a large canvas as he planned to do a full-size nude. He started painting rapidly, realizing he had asked me to maintain a hard pose. That, though, was the least of his challenges: the direction of the sun would change rapidly and when it was gone, that would be the end of it.

In the finished painting, you can see our round wooden bedside table with a blue alarm clock painted in one stroke like a streak of light. Nothing in this picture stands still. You can sense the heat of the sun as it strikes my body. Sunlight blazing through the window ricochets from every surface, bouncing from the sheets and cushions and casting my shadow against the wall behind me. There was no time or need to paint facial features. They looked better left blank and abstract. In fact, Cyril looked through a shard of frosted glass while he was painting to blur what he saw and eliminate too much detail.

MODERN VENUS, c.1963

Oil on canvas, 112 x 71cm (44 x 34in), Private Collection

Cyril draws the curtains and yells at me, 'Don't you fucking move . . . ' He drags in a large canvas and starts to paint. Six decades later I still remember this as my hardest-ever pose. My left arm is lifted above my head and quickly loses sensation. I balance by standing with one foot in front.

My shadow is cast against the wall as I rise from our messy, unmade bed. Our blue alarm clock glitters in the sun on our round table. 'Can we go for a Wimpy when this is done?' I want to know . . . No such luck, we're both too exhausted.

THE RED CHAIRS, BEVIN COURT, 1961
Oil on canvas, 112 x 71cm (44 x 30in), Private Collection

You can see green drapery hiding our folding zedbed on which a brass vase with flowers is perched. The red chairs appear in many of Cyril's pictures of this period. Looking out of the door you glimpse the bathroom window. On the left is a bookcase on top of which stands a plaster-cast portrait of Sylvia, which Cyril modelled in clay. Right in the foreground is a table corner with a yellow book and vase of flowers.

SELF-PORTRAIT WITH HAT, *c.*1968
Oil on canvas, 5˚ x 43.5cm (20 x 17¼in), The Estate of Cyril Mann / courtesy of Piano
Nobile, Robert Travers (Works of Art) Ltd

Cyril is worried. I'm expecting a baby and life is uncertain. Anxiety is etched on
his ageing face

ROSES IN A GLASS VASE, 1963

Oil on canvas, 70 x 53cm (27½ x 20¾in), The Estate of Cyril Mann / courtesy of Piano Nobile, Robert Travers (Works of Art) Ltd

Speed is of the essence. Less is more. Cyril needs to keep up as the sun moves through our room and light effects change instantly, much to his frustration. He paints rapidly, without first sketching, omitting detail and concentrating on the movement of light as it ricochets and bounces off surfaces. 'It's taken me thirty to years to learn what's important in art. Direct painting like this leaves no room for mistakes. It either comes off, or it doesn't,' he grunts in my direction.

Chapter 10

TECHNIQUE

At this stage in his artistic career, Cyril rarely made preliminary sketches. A painting had to be done in one go, with him scooping large gobbets of paint straight from the tin – never tubes – on to his palette, generally using only primaries: red, yellow, Prussian blue, plus black and white, which he mixed with incredible speed and miraculous accuracy into any hue he liked. This way of painting was, he said, far more difficult than 'licking up' a highly realistic nude using fine sable brushes. 'One wrong move with direct painting like mine, and I've ruined it. I want to paint sunlight, not as if it's soaking into the surface, but as a constantly moving and dazzling force, taking precedence over everything.'

Even large works were completed in a few hours, as the sunlight fled before him. But when people asked how long a picture had taken him, he'd reply: thirty-five years. That's how long it had required to develop the technical skill to paint in this way. And there were no second chances. If a painting failed, that was it. He rarely returned to a picture he felt hadn't worked.

Cyril generally painted on rough hessian, creating vigorous textures on stretchers he knocked up himself. He hated the smooth mass-produced texture of fine linen, finding it intimidating and – of course – expensive. Similarly, he disliked sable brushes that allowed fine detail, preferring coarse, hog's-hair brushes large enough to enable him to cover wide areas quickly. He seldom used proper artists' paper for drawing, favouring the surface of brown wrapping paper, and if he didn't have that, newspaper would do.

Cyril's problem, as he said himself, was that he saw too much. He had phenomenal eyesight – considering he had spent much of his life staring at and painting the sun. 'I don't want to paint every hair on a head or leaf on a tree,' he said, knowing that he could never beat a photograph for accuracy. 'There is no way a painter can compete with nature. It is pointless painting every petal of a flower. An artist's role is to transform nature and make others see it in a new way.'

When looking at Cyril's sunlight paintings, a good tip is to half close your eyes. Imagine entering through a door and being dazzled by sunlight streaming through the window. Squinting reduces the glare and helps you to focus.

c.M. 67

Chapter 11

SOCIAL HOUSING

Before I moved in with Cyril, I had no idea what social housing meant. Nor did I understand why living in Bevin Court – named after the Labour politician Ernest Bevin – should carry a stigma. While living at home with my middle-class parents in a small Dutch university town, I had never met people who needed state help to survive. I was mystified why my colleagues at work should raise their eyebrows in disapproval at the idea of me living with a middle-aged man in a *council flat*.

In the year when Lonnie Donegan sang 'My old man's a dustman, he wears a dustman's hat, he wears gorblimey trousers and he lives in a council flat', I took a friend from work to see the block where I had gone to join my beloved. The place looked grim and windswept as we approached, but I spoke up defensively. 'Why is this so bad?'

My friend didn't bother to answer. For her, it was obvious. Middle-class professional families were a rarity in council blocks. True, a commercial artist of sorts lived on our floor with his wife and son, but we never introduced ourselves or got to know them. Mr and Mrs Neville and their schoolgirl daughter were our next-door neighbours. Mrs Neville, a cashier at our local cinema, disapproved of Cyril's and my relationship, but was careful never to say anything that might cause offence. We were reasonably friendly, but once again we never got on to first-name terms.

We did, however, get to know the Bevin Court caretaker, an elderly man whose officious, military manner annoyed Cyril. He was only doing his job, which was not easy! Unruly Teddy boys ran riot in the flats at night, drinking. I'd laugh when

TOWER BLOCK AND COTTAGES, WALTHAMSTOW, c.1967
Lithograph, size unknown, The Estate of Cyril Mann / courtesy of Piano Nobile, Robert Travers (Works of Art) Ltd

Home ownership in England is reserved for the wealthy in the 1960s. To solve the housing crisis, prefabricated high-rise concrete blocks, known as 'streets in the sky', are built for London's rising working-class population. Many are poorly constructed and later demolished. Cyril is fascinated by the contrast of a modern tower block dwarfing derelict Victorian cottages. Walthamstow's cooling towers in the background are demolished in 1969 to make way for the last station on the new Victoria Tube line.

they addressed Cyril as 'Dad'. The lads enjoyed targeting him. One Guy Fawkes nightthey stuck a firework into the pocket of his raincoat, leaving scorch marks where it exploded, causing him a massive shock.

Bevin Court had no front door. But although it was open to the elements, there was an awful lingering smell each morning after the marauding youths had used the lifts as a urinal. A strong smell of Dettol, bleach and carbolic soap permeated the communal areas as cleaners swabbed down the lifts, a task they had to repeat time and again. 'An animal wouldn't foul its nest like that,' moaned Cyril in disgust.

Other than Cyril, few residents appreciated the building's masterful architectural features or the now-famous staircase. He used to make me look up from the bottom of the circular stairwell with its patterns of walkways radiating overhead. 'It's wonderful, Renske,' he'd enthuse. On the left as you entered was a large Picassoesque muralpainted by the architect Lubetkin's collaborator, Peter Yates, and opposite, in its own niche, a full-size bronze bust of Ernest Bevin.

Unfortunately, the bust didn't look much like the Labour politician. The caretaker, concerned that the bronze was turning green with verdigris, had carefully painted the entire portrait black. When Cyril pointed out that this was the wrong approach to restoration, the two men bristled at each other like tomcats! Years later thieves made off with the work, which weighed a ton and would have fetched a good price as scrap.

OPPOSITE
SELF-PORTRAIT WITH HEAD OF SYLVIA, c.1955
Charcoal and chalk drawing on paper, 32 x 51cm (12$^{1}/_{2}$ x 20$^{1}/_{4}$in), The Estate of Cyril Mann / courtesy of Piano Nobile, Robert Travers (Works of Art) Ltd
Cyril's daughter Sylvia by his first wife, Mary, regularly visits her dad in Paul Street. He models her portrait in clay, then casts it in plaster and paints it dark green to resemble bronze. It stands on top of his bookcase and next to his easel and mirror, which catches his ageing face.

Chapter 12

DESTINY BECKONS

As I write, I have before me a gift token presented as a leaving gift to Cyril on 19 February 1960, by his colleagues at Kingsway Day College. Only three months after we met, I had persuaded Cyril to give up teaching and allow me to support him financially, so that he could paint full-time. I felt it was my destiny to help him realize his potential as an artist and persuade a wider public of his unique gifts and originality.

As a teenager, I'd visited the Kröller-Müller Museum near Arnhem, with its outstanding collection of van Gogh paintings and drawings, paintings that would probably never have seen the light of day if it hadn't been for Vincent's younger brother Theo, who recognized his talents and supported him throughout his short life. The paintings in the museum had in turn been bought long before the artist was famous by Helene Kröller-Müller, wife of a wealthy Dutch industrialist. From these examples I had developed the fantasy that I might also one day discover an artist and help him realize his potential. From the moment I first saw Cyril's paintings I was convinced I had discovered the British van Gogh.

PORTRAIT OF SYLVIA, 1957
Oil on canvas, 82 x 57cm (32$\frac{1}{4}$ x 22$\frac{1}{2}$in),
Private Collection

This striking portrait shows Cyril's daughter Sylvia as a slightly sulky, bored teenager shortly before she departed for Keele University. She is holding a book, showing her love of literature; she later became a published author, poet and playwright. Sylvia was similar to her father in many ways, with strong feelings and a talent for the cutting word – and their relationship was tempestuous. Years later, in an afterword to John Russell Taylor's book on Cyril she wrote, 'He was a very difficult man. "Difficult" was the word always tactfully used to describe his irrational rages, which sometimes turned to actual violence, and his tantrums. "Tantrums" is the right word here as sometimes he behaved like a spoilt two-year old child.' Nonetheless, she continued to visit him and keep in touch until the day he died.

Although I was twenty and he was forty-eight, our age difference meant nothing to me. I was eager to learn, and my mind was like a sponge, not only readily absorbing what Cyril was trying to achieve in his art, but acquiring as much and as quickly as possible from his decades of learning as he led me around museums and art galleries. He opened my eyes to art from all periods and every part of the world, from Hokusai's Japanese wood-block prints and the Assyrian lion hunt friezes in the British Museum to the Dutch Old Masters, Cyril's home-grown heroes Turner, Constable, Gainsborough and not forgetting, of course, 'Ol' Mike' (Michelangelo), 'Ol' Vincent' (van Gogh) and 'Daddy Cezanne', his great role models.

I felt I was destined to do what I could to get Cyril's art to a wider audience and for his gifts to be appreciated. And in truth, despite our recurring financial difficulties and hand-to-mouth existence, I never felt any sense of hardship. In spite of the age difference, his energy was boundless compared with mine. I needed eight hours' solid sleep and was always first to feel exhausted, to Cyril's annoyance and frustration. He never wanted to retire before midnight. It was I who felt worn out. He seemed tireless in comparison. I didn't realize then that his insomnia was a symptom of the manic depression with which he was later diagnosed.

One afternoon, a few months into our relationship, I had a terrible premonition that he might not always be there for me. I came home from work to find that Cyril had done a painting while I had been out. This was only to be expected, but the subject matter gave me a nasty jolt.

The painting was of our single bed, empty, with sunlight streaking across the sheets and blankets. It filled me with dread, and I wondered what on earth I would do if Cyril weren't there, cuddling up beside me. I could not imagine anything more awful.

When he asked what I thought of the painting, I was dumbstruck. I could not confess my fears about the empty bed, so I just mumbled, 'Nice.' He growled: 'Why are you damning me with faint praise?'

My premonition, however, proved uncannily accurate, and it makes me wonder if we aren't sometimes given a glimpse of the future. I arrived home the next day to find that Cyril wasn't waiting for me. Normally he would be watching out from the seventh-floor window of our flat, to see me walking down the path to Bevin Court. Today, though, he wasn't there.

I went into the flat – no Cyril – and from the kitchen window I saw a policeman approaching. He had come to give me the bad news: Cyril had collapsed in the street with a perforated ulcer and had been taken to the Royal Free Hospital, then in nearby Gray's Inn Road, for an emergency operation. He had left a message: would I mind telling his daughter Sylvia? Cyril had suffered from stomach ulcers for years and the constant pain had left him weak, ill and short-tempered. Was I going to lose my lover, my soulmate, so soon?

I did what I had been asked and visited the King's Cross office where Sylvia was working as a temp during the university vacation. I wasn't prepared for her reaction. 'I hate my dad,' she said. 'You what?' I asked in disbelief, astonished at her brutal response. I had only known Cyril for a few months and had no idea why Mary, Sylvia's mother, had left him.

Sylvia looked weary and resigned. I didn't want to argue with her, as I was in awe of her. Cyril had spoken with pride about his daughter, telling me how talented she was, winning a scholarship to the City of London School for Girls and subsequently a place at Keele, then the coolest, newest university in the country. When I met her that day, she was in her second year reading English and French and was now back in London for the Easter holiday.

Why did she loathe him so much at this stage in life? I had begun to realize that Cyril could be very difficult, but I loved him body and soul and nothing could change that at the time.

After graduating from Keele, Sylvia married Howard Dewhirst and had two daughters, Emma and Sarah. She had a third child, Gideon, with another partner, Robert Daniels. Gideon became a high-flyer in the diplomatic service and has become passionately interested in his grandfather's paintings.

Chapter 13

LOVE STORY

Here are some extracts from a letter I wrote to Cyril on 3 April 1960, when he was in the Royal Free Hospital recovering from his perforated ulcer operation. Note that I still called him Mr Mann, despite the fact we were living together as lovers.

Dear Mr Mann

How dreadful that I can't come to see you tonight. You don't like the evenings in hospital, do you? Well, I don't like the evenings in Bevin Court. Why? Because 108 Bevin Court is not complete when you're not here. You are so much my man in body and soul that I simply cannot do without you.

When I'm writing to you, and from time to time, I'm looking at your paintings, I feel you are so near to me. I love you Mr Mann. I want to tell you over and over again I love you, and I pray that I will be your woman for all your life. I realize that I have not much to offer you; no beauty, no money, only my love and I hope one day to prove to you that my love is worth more than beauty or money. You have everything I always wanted: you are an artist, you are my husband, my friend, my love, everything. When you leave the hospital I will ask for a day off. I will stuff the flat with flowers for you.

Cyril had first been plagued by ulcers in 1948, when some of his London bomb site paintings were shown in the exhibition 'Artists of Fame and Promise' at the prestigious Wildenstein Gallery in Bond Street. The director and curator, a Colonel Jack Beddington, had taken ages to decide whether or not to include the paintings: Cyril's paintings may have been masterpieces, but three years after the war people needed cheering up, not reminding of the Blitz. The uncertainty had caused Cyril enormous anxiety and stress. By the time the gallery agreed to accept them, poor Cyril was on his knees with worry.

The stomach ulcers caused paroxysms of pain every time Cyril had a meal. He avoided alcohol, fearing that it would burn his stomach lining. He was a chain-smoker, which didn't help. The years of professional neglect, frustration and financial anxiety,

SUNLIT LANDSCAPE, *c*.1950
Oil on canvas, 35.5 x 51cm (14 x 20in), Private Collection, photograph by Daniel Colbert
Cyril loved painting landscapes but had few opportunities to venture into the countryside,
as he never learned to drive a car. He probably did this picture during one summer holiday,
staying at the Artists' Rest Home in rural Rickmansworth.

combined with teaching, had worn him down. Although he had been a popular teacher, he said that he 'hated training others to become failures'. To compound his dejected state, his mother and sister had died a few months earlier and he had almost lost the will to live.

Now imagine the contrast when he awoke from the emergency operation at the Royal Free. He was pain-free for the first time in decades. I had already promised to look after him and free him from the constant nagging of financial woes. I knew that I could always earn a living as shorthand-typing jobs were plentiful. Further, I promised I would go out and sell his pictures, something he was sceptical about, but I was confident the world would soon appreciate his unique qualities as an artist.

But first of all, before getting back to painting, he went to convalesce at the Artists' Rest Home in Rickmansworth, founded in 1929 by a wealthy amateur painter, Francis William Reckitt, of the Reckitt & Colman company, to benefit artists who were 'too poor to afford holidays or time to convalesce'.

Cyril had spent many summers there. He was given a comfortable room, painting facilities and three meals a day – meals he could now eat and enjoy after the operation. The only problem, at least so far as we were concerned, was that at the time it was strictly men only. Later, female artists were also admitted.

I lodged at the Swan Inn nearby so I could visit him for tea. The only other resident of the Home, an ancient artist, sat dozing in an armchair. He opened his eyes as I approached and shouted, 'It's Nefertiti!' 'No,' said Cyril. 'She's my Lolita.'

PEAT BOGS IN CONNEMARA, 1959
Oil on canvas, 39 x 49cm (15¼ x 19in), The Estate of Cyril Mann / courtesy of Piano
Nobile, Robert Travers (Works of Art) Ltd

Cyril's holiday in Ireland, travelling on a Lambretta with Sylvia riding pillion, is
not a success: she abandons her dad and returns to London on her own. He
continues his journey alone, keeping art stuff in a sidecar and staying in B&Bs.
He roams around Connemara painting lonely peatbogs reflecting the sky.

Chapter 14

THE STRUGGLE BEGINS

With Cyril home from convalescence, our struggle to sell his paintings began in earnest. 'It's easy enough painting pictures,' he said. 'The hard thing is selling the fuckers.' He flatly refused to show paintings to galleries. 'They're not interested in art, only money, and I won't give them the satisfaction of rejecting me. They can't do what I do. They don't know what I know,' he insisted.

The previous summer, 1959, he had bought a second-hand Lambretta scooter with sidecar, planning a painting holiday in Ireland and taking his teenage daughter Sylvia with him. They fetched up in Connemara, which Cyril described as a paradise. 'You should have seen the donkeys with their long toenails. It rained all the time, but when it stopped, you could see the sky reflected in the peat bogs. The Irish only eat bacon and potatoes. They're all bonkers, incurable romantics.'

It is perhaps significant that on this holiday, where they argued all the time, Sylvia rode pillion while her father's art materials were kept in the sidecar. In the end, they returned home separately as they bickered with each other so much. Still, Cyril had an armful of Irish landscapes that he framed himself, each with a simple strip surroundknown in the art world as a baguette. Now back from the Rest Home and with his optimism renewed, he visited the Red Lion pub in Bowling Green Lane, Clerkenwell, whose owner was Irish. When told about Cyril's paintings, he immediately offered him his walls to show the paintings. It sounded ideal: Irish pub, Irish clientele, near where we lived in Bevin Court.

Cyril, however, wasn't yet fully recovered from his major operation and was emaciated and tired. He looked worn out, having to frame his pictures, cart them to the Red Lion and hang them. But his hopes were high, as were mine. He might even sell a few and restore our flagging fortunes.

The private view was a raucous affair with plenty of drinkers in the pub, but not a single buyer. No one even seemed to notice Cyril's Irish pictures. We walked home deflated. The paintings were up for weeks, but there wasn't a single sale. Cyril refused from then on to show his paintings in restaurants or pubs. People, he argued, would get used to seeing them as part of the furniture and the price tickets and labels would simply disappear.

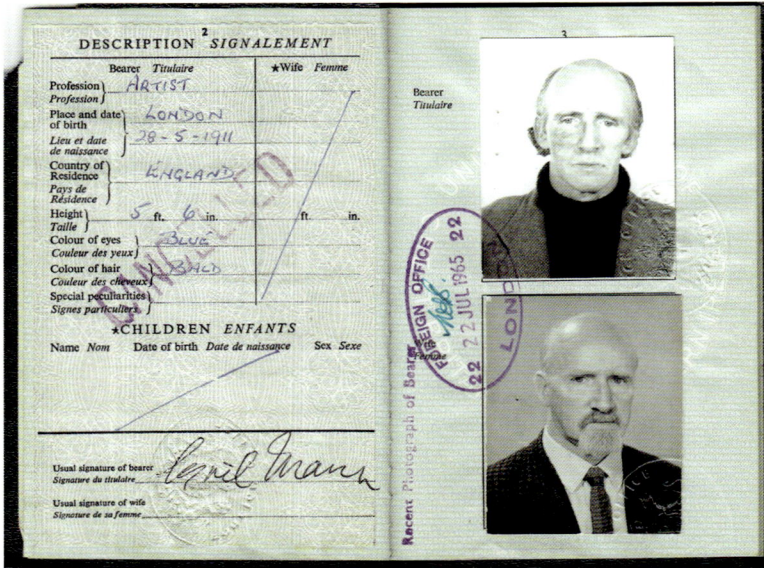

Summoned to meet my parents in 1960, Cyril must apply for a passport. He has never flown in a plane before. His passport photo, taken days after a serious nervous breakdown, shows him with a black eye inflicted by the ambulance men who came to section him in London's Royal Free Hospital's psychiatric unit. In the second passport photograph, a few years later, he has fully recovered.

Meanwhile, the beaten-up Lambretta was parked somewhere in the street near Bevin Court. Months later Cyril invited me for a ride on the back. His recklessness and bad temper were terrifying. I couldn't wait to get off. He never learned to drive a car, and in later years, when I could drive and had a company car, he was the world's worst back-seat driver. 'Keep close to the car in front, so other cars can't overtake,' he used to order me, while doing seventy miles an hour on a motorway. I insisted that Cyril sell his Lambretta. It would have been the death of him if I hadn't.

The disastrous exhibition, meanwhile, became the trigger for a serious nervous breakdown, which nearly killed us both.

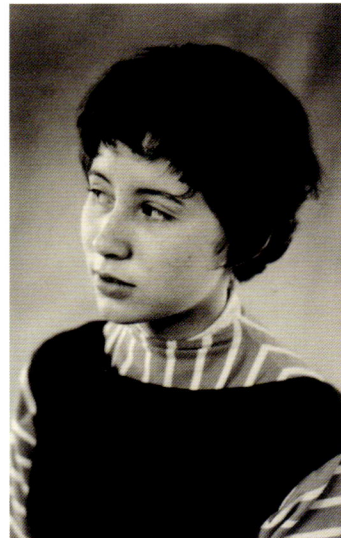

Chapter 15

BREAKDOWN

Is there any greater torture, I wonder, than being kept awake when you desperately need to sleep? I crept into bed very late one night, but Cyril had other ideas. His mind – and loud voice blasting into my ears – went into overdrive. He was going to design the greatest mural the world had ever seen, starting right there and then.

Whenever he spotted me dozing, he yanked my arm and ordered me to help with the preparations He taped together sheets of newspaper, placed them down on the carpet, then used a box of drawing pins to tack the entire sheet to the carpet. Using charcoal and crayons, he set to work, sketching not only on the newspaper sheets, but frantically writing notes on the walls. 'Why do you waste half your life, sleeping?' he demanded of me angrily.

The flat was in chaos, a reflection of Cyril's fevered and agonized mind. He ranted and raved endlessly, not just at me but at his artistic heroes, Ol' Mike, Ol' Vincent and Daddy Cezanne.

As for me, I was petrified of the tacks on the floor since I had no slippers. But after twenty-four hours, when he virtually kept me a prisoner in the flat, I could stand no more: I just had to sleep. The flat was awash with tranquillizers and sleeping pills, and in desperation, I took some. I had no idea what or how many. I had to sleep and this time I would make sure he couldn't wake me.

I have no further memories of that night. I blacked out and awoke in the Royal Free Hospital, where Cyril had so recently undergone his perforated-ulcer operation. Sitting next to my bed was Basil Bernstein, later a celebrated sociology professor, then a teaching colleague of Cyril's at Kingsway Day College. He and his wife Marion were good friends of Cyril's who had supported him and bought his paintings. I've no idea how he came to be sitting there; at the time I just accepted it. 'Go home, Renske,' he urged. 'Go back to Holland, for God's sake. Cyril will never change. He's incurable.'

Cyril must have noticed my parlous state, as he was sane enough, at least, to call an ambulance. But when it came, as I heard later, the medics refused to let him come with me. Infuriated, he attacked a policeman and kicked an ambulance man. Someone fought back and gave Cyril a black eye. A separate ambulance was then summoned for Cyril and, on arrival, the man in charge of the Royal Free psychiatric ward, nurse Jimmy Porteous, ordered Cyril to be locked in a padded cell, strapping him into a straitjacket and admitting him into the mental unit.

Meanwhile his Irish pictures languished in the Red Lion pub, unsold and unloved. While he was incarcerated in the psychiatric ward, he could not fetch them himself and I had no idea how to get them back to Bevin Court on my own.

MIXED FLOWERS IN A BRASS VASE, 1961
Oil on board, 100 x 75cm (39^1/$_4$ x 29^1/$_2$in), Collection the late Dr and Mrs Hardisty

In this large exuberant flower painting, Cyril lets go, using paint lavishly and instinctively. He is no longer content to imitate nature but wants us to see what he sees as important.

Chapter 16

BACK TO NORMALITY

Cyril came back from hospital subdued, depressed and drugged to the eyeballs. His psychiatrist would not release him until he had promised to take his prescription drugs, yes, all of them. 'These tranquillizers suppress my libido,' he grumbled to me.

Not knowing the meaning of the word 'libido', I let that pass. I was thankful that Cyril was now calm. Perhaps, though, he was a little too calm? I'd had a good rest while he was in the psychiatric hospital for a couple of weeks. Now, maybe, life could start again. We had still only known each other for a few months, and already I felt as if I had been plunged into a Jacobean drama.

I hoped, with luck, that life would pick up, with us both feeling better. But was Cyril quite back to normal? The pills not only reduced his libido but dampened his creativity. Before long he started reducing his dose strictly against the doctors' orders. He argued that if he continued taking the recommended dose, they would stop him painting, and for Cyril that would be a fate worse than death.

We slowly gathered up the pieces of our already shattered lives. I was still passionately in love with him and did what I could to help him return to normality. This started with a clean-up of the flat. We swept up the mass of newspapers on the floor and picked the tacks off the carpet. Cyril repainted the walls he had graffitied. We then decided that the Victorian leather armchairs took up too much space and had to go. Then − wonderful treat − we bought an up-to-the minute G-plan three-piece suite. It was cheap, probably because nobody else would have been mad enough to buy it.

The chairs had bright red upholstery, which would have been too garish for most people's tastes, but the vibrant colour excited Cyril visually. He immediately asked me to pose. By now he had overcome the soporific effects of the tranquillizers and was inspired all over again.

We sat down and made a deal together. Cyril had £310 in his bank account inherited from his mother, who had died just before we met. The legacy would provide our safety net, not to be touched for day-to-day living. Any money he made from his paintings would go straight into this account. The money I earned from my secretarial work would be used to live on. My pay came weekly in cash, in small brown envelopes minus tax deductions. The little envelope would be in a communal place, so that we could help ourselves without asking, until the money ran out.

A commemorative plaque (see page 50) celebrates Cyril's artistic achievements from 1956 to 1964 in Bevin Court. Considered one of Britain's great post-war modernist buildings, the block was designed by Russian architect Berthold Lubetkin. Its sculptural staircase is a must-see for architectural students.

It was all a huge relief to Cyril. Now that we had worked out how to apportion our money, we bought a folding zedbed with room for two. No more sleeping together in a single bed. We were gradually turning Cyril's untidy bachelor flat into a home.

After the arrival of our red chairs and zedbed, we went through a happy, peaceful phase. Yes, Cyril often cheated on his tranquillizers and forgot (or forgot on purpose) to take them, but he kept himself in control. I now worked part-time so that I could look after him properly. We were always short of cash, but as we were used to being poor, it didn't bother us.

NORTH VIEW FROM BEVIN COURT, 1960
Oil on canvas, 60 x 51cm (23^1/$_2$ x 20in), The Estate of Cyril Mann / courtesy of Piano Nobile, Robert Travers (Works of Art) Ltd

Cyril painted many views from our flat on the seventh floor of Bevin Court, capturing different weather conditions.

SOUTH VIEW WITH ST. PAUL'S FROM BEVIN COURT, 1960

Oil on board,
51 x 75cm
(20^1/$_8$ x 29^1/$_2$in),
Private Collection

He watched me walking down the path coming home from work, eager to show me what he had painted that day.

Meanwhile, the divorce from Cyril's first wife, Mary, was proceeding. They had lived apart for ten years and while he paid her no maintenance, he had contributed to Sylvia's upkeep from his modest, insecure part-time teaching income. Sylvia was now nineteen and on a full grant which she supplemented with holiday jobs. There were no arguments and no settlements to be made, as neither Mary nor Cyril owned any property or investments.

Mary and I smiled at each other when I went with Cyril to the divorce court. To me she looked a sweet old lady, at least Cyril's age. And so began an unlikely friendship that lasted until her death. Mary never let on what she thought of Cyril marrying a twenty-year-old from Holland.

In the twenty years I lived with Cyril I never heard him or Mary utter one word against each other. She confessed that she had been too meek and should have stood up to him but didn't dare, because he bullied her. He was insensitive, putting it mildly. I doubt if Mary knew that Cyril had several love affairs. He had considered leaving her, but in the end she took that fateful step and walked out in the middle of the night. Cyril was bereft: he had lost not only a lovely wife, but his brilliant teenage daughter, Sylvia.

THREE OF FIVE STUDIES OF MARY MANN, *c.*1950

Ink, chalk, watercolour, (left to right) 28 x 21.5cm (11 x 8¹/₂in); 27.8 x 21.5cm (11 x 8¹/₂in); 31.7 x 23.9cm (12¹/₂ x 9¹/₂in), Private Collection

Cyril painted few portraits of his first wife, probably because Mary worked to help keep the family afloat financially.

OPPOSITE
SELF-PORTRAIT WITH PALETTE AND BRUSHES, 1962

Oil on canvas, 91.2 x 53.4cm (35⁷/₈ x 21¹/₈in), The Estate of Cyril Mann / courtesy of Piano Nobile, Robert Travers (Works of Art) Ltd

When I'm away during the day, he wears denim overalls and enjoys using paint lavishly. For the first time in his life he doesn't worry about the cost.

Chapter 17

A DAY AT THE PARK

Worryingly, there had been no picture sales for ages. Then I had a bright idea. 'I'll take a few of your paintings to Hyde Park Corner and sell them there.' I knew that many artists put their work up on the railings to sell at weekends. Cyril looked horrified. 'Are you mad?' No, I wasn't mad. Just determined.

The following Saturday, Cyril walked me to the No. 19 bus stop with a few paintings neatly tied up. He refused to come with me and shook his head at what he saw as my obstinate foolishness. In those days, you didn't have to pay to put up paintings on the railings. It was all unlicensed and unregulated. Anybody could put up pictures and sit by them, hoping for a sale from passers-by. But among serious artists, the whole idea of selling paintings 'at Hyde Park' was a joke. Cyril wanted nothing to do with it.

Before moving to their present pitch at Bayswater Road, the outdoor picture stalls were situated near Hyde Park Corner, where I stepped off the bus. There were no supervisors. It was strictly a case of first come, first served. As I was early, I quickly found a gap on the railings.

Unprepared and clueless, I had brought nothing to hang my pictures with. Others had come with string and what looked like butcher's hooks. I leant my pictures against the railings where they were too low down for anybody to see properly.

As I looked around, I could see why Cyril had been so reluctant: the standard of the pictures was woeful. There were acres of garish landscapes and abstracts, plus endless portraits of green Chinese ladies imitating Vladimir Tretchikoff, the dreaded king of kitsch, and pictures of big-eyed toddlers with tears running down their cheeks. Surely nobody who liked this crud could be remotely interested in Cyril's paintings.

Nor were they. I sat there while passers-by cast barely a glance at my offerings. Eventually, however, one young man took pity on me, a young Irishman who said he had come from Dublin and was scratching a living as a window dresser and pub

PORTRAIT OF ERNEST GROOME, 1971
Oil on canvas, 183 x 122cm (72 x 48in), The Estate of Cyril Mann / courtesy of Piano Nobile, Robert Travers (Works of Art) Ltd

I met Ernest Groome – aspiring artist and pub entertainer recently arrived from Dublin – on Hyde Park Corner in 1960. He helped put Cyril's pictures on the railings, raised my spirits and made me laugh. He and his wife, Dorothy, became lifelong friends, who put up with Cyril's rants and temper tantrums.

VIEW OF THE THAMES AGAINST THE SUN, 1952
Charcoal and chalk on paper, 32 x 46cm (12½ x 18in), Private Collection

Cyril saw himself as a successor to the great English Romantic painter J.M.W. Turner (1775–1851), sharing a lifelong obsession with dynamic light effects.

entertainer before – he hoped – his own career as an artist took off. His name was Ernest Groome, and he scrounged around for hooks and string, and swiftly put up my pictures on the railings.

He looked admiringly at the paintings: 'These are bloody good.' Clearly, he thought I was the artist. I told him they were the work of a much older artist called Cyril Mann; by now my spirits were low. Cyril had been right. Taking his pictures to Hyde Park had been a ridiculous idea.

Ernest decided to cheer me up with his pub entertainer routine, 'playing the spoons', making clip-clopping rhythmic noises, followed by a repertoire of beautiful birdsong, done whistling through his fingers. Finally, he picked up his guitar and, with an Irish lilt, sang a Spanish-sounding tune which ended with the ridiculous refrain, 'Manuel, close the door.' I had never heard the song before – or since – but I was entranced. The lovely Ernest had lifted me out of my dejected mood. Then he turned to me and said, 'Will you come out with me on Thursday?' I can't, sorry, I told him. 'I'm getting married that day.'

When they met later, Cyril and Ernest struck up a friendship that was to last for the next twenty years. But Ernie wasn't the only important friend we made that afternoon.

While Ernie had cheered me up considerably, by the end of the afternoon there had been no picture sales. A few people had shown interest, but most passed by without a glance as I waited for Cyril to pick me up. The pictures were heavy and unwieldy and without help I would have struggled to get them home.

Then I spotted a well-dressed, middle-aged couple strolling towards me, wearing grim expressions that suggested they were utterly horrified by the art they were seeing. But the moment they set eyes on Cyril's paintings, they stopped dead in their tracks. And I could read their thoughts: 'Decent art at last!'

As this smart and clearly affluent couple looked carefully through Cyril's paintings, talking animatedly, I could see my husband-to-be trundling along the road, looking sheepish and chewing on what I knew was a jelly baby; he'd given up smoking after his emergency operation, and I bought him sweets every day, hoping they would lessen the agony of nicotine withdrawal and help keep him stable. He was embarrassed at seeing his treasured paintings exhibited among these awful daubs.

The couple introduced themselves as Michael and Sylvia Leibson; he was a doctor, she a sculptor. I explained that I'd brought Cyril's pictures to Hyde Park because we were desperately hard up and I'd do anything to get a sale. Then I introduced Cyril, who was gathering up his paintings. The Leibsons didn't bat an eyelid at our obvious age difference. Sylvia, instead, said, 'Why don't you come to our house this evening with a few more paintings? I'll invite a few friends and they might buy.'

So that same evening we gathered together a portfolio and a bundle of paintings, and once again took the No. 19 bus, this time to Aberdeen Park, a private road in Highbury, where Michael and Sylvia lived in a huge Victorian house. We admired Sylvia's portrait sculpture and looked around their impressive collection of pictures. Other guests soon arrived and by the end of the evening Cyril had sold pictures not only to Sylvia and Mike, but to many of their friends. 'We eat again,' he said.

Cyril first painted the talented young Irish artist in 1961, and they became close. Ernest married Dorothy, a theatre nurse and the perfect artist's wife who supported him financially. They had two beautiful sons, Breffni and Ffion, and – even better from our point of view – they bought two of Cyril's Irish paintings, breaking the spell of that disastrous exhibition a few months earlier.

Cyril did this life-size portrait of Ernie (see page 78) a decade later. Unusually for him, he produced a small-scale preparatory oil sketch of the composition. It was painted at night, so the red lamp shade behind Ernest picks up the colour of his shirt, casting a strong 'solid shadow' against the wall behind him.

The following year, the two friends travelled to Rome together. 'I could have strangled him many times,' confessed Ernie on their return. They visited Michelangelo's Sistine Chapel in the Vatican, which left Cyril underwhelmed. 'Ol' Mike's painting is overrated,' he complained. 'But what a hero to climb all that scaffolding and do that huge amount of physical labour all by himself.'

RECLINING NUDE IN SUNLIGHT, 1962

Oil on canvas, 99 x 84cm (39 x 33in), Private Collection

Cyril omits detail and only wants to render light as a dynamic force. With large hog's-hair paintbrushes, he rapidly covers the canvas, focusing on the way that sunlight falls and reflects on my nude body as it speeds through our room.

Chapter 18

LEONARD COTTRELL

Mike and Sylvia Leibson had a lodger living at the top of their house: Leonard Cottrell, the best-selling author of the 1953 book about ancient Crete, *The Bull of Minos*.

University archaeologists tended to look down on Leonard as he was not formally trained. But unlike them, he had earned a fortune from his blockbusters about ancient civilizations. Leonard was determined to spend his money on two things: an Aston Martin and art. We were very happy about the latter and invited him for dinner.

The evening turned out slightly differently from expected.

For many years, Cyril had loved budgies and usually kept one in Bevin Court. Soon after the war, budgerigars became the pet of choice, or perhaps of necessity, in many London households. Lack of space and the advent of high-rise flats prevented the ownership of larger animals, which were often not allowed under the terms of the tenancy.

Cyril had a budgie called Joey who would sit on his shoulder or on his bald head as he was painting. He would eat from my plate and peck to wake us up in the morning. Little white blobs of budgie poo often appear on Cyril's paintings, as Joey was never kept inside his cage.

ABOVE **SCULPTURE OF BUDGIE, c.1958**
Reclaimed stone, height 26cm (10¼in), Collection Renske Mann

Cyril's favourite budgie, perches on his head when he paints and eats from the side of his dinner plate. It's only ever caged at night. The little bird comes to a sorry end in the jaws of a cat. Cyril is inconsolable. He carves this tribute to his feathered friend from a stone found on a nearby bomb site.

As we sat down to dinner with Leonard on our red chairs, in flew Joey. He circled round the room and then fell down dead on Leonard's lap. Cyril and I were in floods of tears. Joey, or Budgie as he was also known, had simply died of old age but had chosen a bad time to do it. Thankfully, Leonard was undeterred. He bought two magnificent paintings, a reclining nude against white sheets, showing our round table with a yellow tablecloth, and a large flower painting.

Cyril had carved a sculpture of one of his budgies before I met him, when he was first living in Bevin Court. He used a piece of stone that he found on one of the many bomb sites nearby. As well as being a painter, Cyril was an accomplished sculptor, but there were too many complaints from the neighbours about the noise when he was chipping away, so he did fewer stone carvings than he would have liked

AGAINST THE SUN, *c.*1950
Oil on canvas, 50 x 60cm (19$\frac{1}{2}$ x 23$\frac{1}{2}$in), The Estate of Cyril Mann / courtesy of Piano Nobile, Robert Travers (Works of Art) Ltd

Cyril painted few pictures from imagination, preferring to work from direct observation. In this rare example he's inspired by the comic figure of Don Quixote.

Chapter 19

JACK BERNFIELD

Through the Leibsons we met Jack Bernfield, an eminent doctor and consultant physician who shared an unfortunate trait with Cyril: they were both insomniacs. Jack dedicated his life to the NHS at Bethnal Green Hospital, an acute hospital where many of his near-destitute patients were East Enders of Jewish descent, like Jack himself.

As a bachelor, Jack had little time to care for himself. So many grateful patients gave him Bri-Nylon shirts, popular in the 1960s and perfect for his lifestyle: drip-dry and no need to iron! Shame, I thought: Jack was a distinguished, handsome man who dressed in smart navy suits, but these semi-transparent shirts let him down. With crass insensitivity, I told him so Jack took no notice: wearing those shirts was his only way to acknowledge his patients' generosity.

I guessed he was about the same age as Cyril. Having no concept of time, he would often turn up very late in the evening at Bevin Court. As we had no bedroom, I could not escape the banter, laughter and arguments between them. After midnight, he would finally decide to catch a night bus home. Where or how he lived, in a flat or a house, we had no idea.

Was he gay or straight? We didn't care either way and it was better not to know. Homosexuality was illegal then and in the upper echelons of the medical profession, it could have damaged his reputation. All that mattered was that he was kind. 'Why don't you come over a few hours earlier, Jack?' I once timidly suggested. 'There are more planes in the sky than buses on the road,' he replied, blaming his late arrivals on the London transport, which had deteriorated when trolley buses were withdrawn in 1962.

One evening when he arrived well past my bedtime, I asked irritably: 'Why aren't you married?' Quick as a flash, he replied: 'Because you're already married, Renske.' He continued: 'When that old bastard there pops off, we'll walk off into the sunset together.' This ridiculous notion became an in-joke between us that he kept up for months. The minute he set foot in the door, Jack would rush to grab Cyril's pulse and place his hand on his forehead, checking his temperature. 'Damn it, still going strong,' he would grunt.

When Cyril had taught me the rudiments of chess, Jack challenged me to a game: 'I'll play blind,' he said. 'I'll turn my back, so I can't see the board. Cyril will talk me through your moves. I was junior chess champion of England once,' he warned.

Needless to say, there was neither rhyme nor reason to my opening and subsequent moves. Jack was flummoxed, but not for long. He soon realized my knowledge of the game was negligible.

On another evening we went to a pub where I was shocked to discover that Jack had a problem: he was a compulsive gambler. With his jacket- and trouser pockets stuffed with coins, he made a beeline for the one-armed bandits – slot machines that only took coppers in those days.

While keeping up the chat, Jack unceasingly pulled the handle and inserted the coins. Random symbols – usually of fruit, hence the name 'fruit machine' – would spin around and when they stopped on identical symbols, handfuls of coins would clatter out. Jack could not resist this brainless pastime. He inserted the coins until his pockets were empty.

Later that year, when he came to visit us one evening, his usual banter began again: 'Are you feeling OK, Cyril, let me take your pulse?' Then his mood suddenly turned sombre. 'I'm terrified of dying,' I overheard him saying to Cyril. Did he have a premonition, I wondered? We knew that he worked himself half to death in the hospital, but he was always relaxed, bright and happy during his visits. What made him say this?

Weeks later and completely out of the blue, Jack's only brother telephoned us with shocking news. Jack had died suddenly after a massive heart attack. Nothing could have saved him. He was still in his fifties.

I was the only woman at Jack's miserable funeral in the Jewish cemetery. I didn't know it wasn't customary for women other than close relatives to attend. Cyril and I followed his coffin to his grave, weeping for our friend.

Months later we had another phone call from Jack's brother, telling us that Jack had remembered us in his will and left us £100, a small fortune at the time. It would have been more, his brother confessed, had it not been for his gambling habit.

Chapter 20

MARRIED

The decree absolute on Cyril's divorce came through on 24 August 1960. It was my twenty-first birthday. A week later, on September 1st, we were married. I didn't invite my parents, colleagues or friends from the YWCA hostel. There were just the four of us at Finsbury Town Hall, Cyril and me and our two witnesses, an old friend of Cyril's, Reggie Rouse, Finsbury's head librarian, and Dr John Abernethy, our young local GP. Our wedding lunch took place in a most unusual institution, the Brush & Palette Club in Bayswater, a place we had encountered through the strangest circumstances.

As we were packing up Cyril's paintings that fateful afternoon by the Hyde Park railings, we were accosted by a tall, bearded, handsome man, probably in his thirties. His name, he said, was John and he needed urgent help. Opportunities to see nudity in public places were few and far between then. Strip clubs were considered seedy and very strictly regulated. Life classes for artists, however, were accepted so John had turned a basement in nearby Bayswater into a members-only restaurant and club, where, on paying a small fee, members could have a meal and then, if they felt like it, sketch pretty naked young girls.

Fearing that he might lose his restaurant licence, John wanted Cyril to help him turn his club into a proper artists' destination: by hanging Cyril's pictures on the walls and by Cyril doing some drawing and tutoring there himself.

With the unfortunate Red Lion exhibition still raw in his mind, Cyril wasn't keen. He had decided he never wanted to show paintings in a pub or restaurant again. 'What's your lighting?' he asked John, realizing the venue was a basement without natural daylight. When told that it was candles, Cyril shook his head. 'Sorry, no. Candles are awful for paintings. The smoke leaves a dirty residue on the paint surface. Just look at what happens to art in churches.'

But John wouldn't take no for an answer. He invited us to come for free meals with a couple of friends whenever we felt like it. Now you're talking, we thought. We went, of course.

So our wedding lunch with our two witnesses took place at the Brush & Palette, generously provided by John and his staff. It was roast pigeon – I squeamishly hoped we weren't consuming birds captured in Trafalgar Square – a dish I had never eaten before, or since come to that.

GOLDEN TORSO, 1961

Oil on canvas, 59.5 x 49.5cm (23½ x 19½in), Ben Uri Gallery and Museum, London, presented by Alistair McAlpine

When the author and art critic John Berger sees this picture, he recommends it for the Granada TV Art Collection. There's just one snag: the painting has already been snapped up by another collector. John Berger reluctantly chooses another picture for his sponsor. We're thrilled: it means selling two instead of one.

No photos were taken of the occasion, there were no flowers, no wedding cake and certainly no wedding dress, but I was now, in the eyes of others, a respectably married woman. Our wedding was, in fact, very similar to Cyril's earlier one with Mary just before the war. That time, friends told me, Cyril went out in the street and accosted two passers-by to be witnesses.

I was still utterly besotted with Cyril, but why? Maybe we look for 'parent figures' in our lives, but Cyril was nothing like my parents. Perhaps the answer was simply that my admiration for him as an artist knew no bounds: I was in love with his paintings, too.

He was slow to fall for me, partly because he was so ill before his ulcer operation, when he had tried hard to persuade me to move in with his ex-girlfriend Alison. Yet once Cyril did fall in love with me, he was mine, body and soul. 'I'll match you love for love,' he promised. He meant it.

For my part, I believed I was destined to take care of him. I wanted to give Cyril a new lease of life, give him the opportunity to go back to painting without distractions and anxieties about money. He had had some barren years artistically before we met, when he was ill and had to travel to Nottingham to care for his sick mother and dying sister.

There was no question of us having children at this point and we took the necessary precautions. We could not afford a family and the one-bedroom Bevin Court flat was certainly not suitable. But Cyril had promised that he would never deny me a baby, if and when I thought the time was right.

With life looking up, we made frequent trips to the Brush & Palette. The long basement was divided into three sections. In front of the main restaurant was a small area where members could draw. Behind this, curtained off, was a chair on which a model sat motionless. The curtain opened and lo and behold, there was a stark-naked teenager, pubic hair and all. It was all coy and strictly no touch, but instead of pulling in genuine artists, the club quickly attracted the dirty-mac brigade.

Cyril chose a few paintings to hang on the walls, instantly making the Brush & Palette look like a gallery rather than just a seedy nightclub. He also started sketching some of the girls during their static half-hour poses and helping a handful of club members by drawing alongside them.

We enjoyed ourselves, made a few picture sales and met interesting people. Before long the licensing authorities decided that nothing illegal was going on and there were no more worries on that score. It was a great place to meet our friends. Musical entertainment was provided by an overweight, middle-aged tenor who had had occasional small roles at Sadler's Wells. Going through his usual repertoire one evening – 'La Donna e Mobile' from *Rigoletto* was a favourite – the bulky singer saw the friends we were expecting coming downstairs.

He stopped mid-note and stared in amazement to see Anna Pollak, the leading mezzo-soprano, accompanied by her lifelong companion, Erica Marx, the wealthy benefactor who had financed a trust fund that enabled Cyril to study at the Royal Academy Schools and in Paris before the war. Having sung in the chorus as Anna took centre-stage at Sadler's Wells, our Brush & Palette tenor almost kissed the floor as she walked in.

What shocked me at the time was the open physical affection between Erica and Anna. Cyril whispered: 'They're lesbians!' How I envied such a relationship, one without fear and with what looked like total contentment. When I told a friend how I felt, she said: 'You've found a father. Are you now looking for a mother as well?'

Of course, my friend was being facetious, but she struck a nerve. As a child and teenager, I had serious and painful crushes on girls, which never unfurled into sexual relationships. With the exception of my boundless admiration for Cyril, I loved and idolized many of my women friends.

One afternoon Vic Singh arrived with a new camera to photograph the view from our flat; Bevin Court was then still one of the tallest buildings in London. And he made what he soon realized was a mistake: offering to pose for Cyril. The poor chap had seriously underestimated how exhausting modelling could be, especially in a standing pose. He stood, one foot raised, with his elbow resting across his knee while stretching one arm towards the bookcase in order to stay upright and keep in balance. It is a crowded composition done in a small, crowded room, with artist and model working in close proximity. Sweat soon dripped off Vic's forehead, exacerbated by the hot, bright lamplight above.

With its pure, vivid colours, this painting is more than a portrait: it is a picture of a 'moment'. Loose brush strokes convey a sense of movement, recording not only the young man – one of Cyril's favourite students – but also evoking Cyril's own turbulent and emotional personality. There is no need for narrative content. The reciprocity between artist and model says it all. Vic was gorgeous, both in looks and personality. At this stage, none of us had any idea that he would become famous in his own right as a photographer of pop stars.

MY STUDENT, VIC SINGH, *c.*1962

Oil on board, 91.5 x 61cm (36 x 24in), Private Collection

You may remember the handsome lad I saw in the art class on the evening I met Cyril. Vic Singh's mother was Austrian and his father an Indian politician who later married Svetlana Alliluyeva, daughter of Russian dictator Joseph Stalin. As the 1960s progressed Vic became a photographer and a figure in the psychedelic London scene, best known for shooting the cover of Pink Floyd's *The Piper at the Gates of Dawn*.

Chapter 21

A STEEP LEARNING CURVE

Before long, I realized that I wanted to better myself, to become more interesting to people in the art world, more of an equal to Cyril, who had lived a full life before he met me.

First, I wanted to learn to cook. Cyril had taught me the basics, but I needed proper lessons and he agreed to let me attend evening classes. It may sound odd that I felt I needed permission, but Cyril was the boss in our relationship – certainly at this stage – no question! For the first four years of our relationship, I had no life independent of Cyril, and nor did I want or seek any.

Our kitchen at Bevin Court was tiny and doubled as a prep room for Cyril's art. There was no fridge and no washing machine – we used a local launderette when we could afford it – and just a little blue Formica table and two wooden chairs. On our Baby Belling cooker animal glue pellets, for 'sizing' canvases, would be found simmering in a saucepan. We must have been the neighbours from hell: if it wasn't the noise from Cyril chipping away at stones, it was the acrid smells from the kitchen, fumes from turps, oils and other solvents that made you feel dizzy.

One day Cyril came home with a bucket of London clay from a building site. He was fond of doing pottery and even taught it for a while. The clay, he explained, had to be washed first and the only place to do this was in our bath. 'You won't be able to use it for a while,' he warned. After about a week I was desperate, but the bath was still out of bounds. Instead, Cyril took me to the communal baths in Ironmonger Row. We were each given a towel and directed to separate cubicles. It was bliss.

My cookery evening classes started promisingly enough. We were told to bring corned beef, a potato, onion, carrot, lard and flour for pastry. I was proud of the Cornish pasty I produced.

And in other ways I gradually became more confident of my own abilities. Our next-door neighbour, Mrs Neville, worked in a local cinema where she smuggled us in with free tickets to see films. From Cyril, I learned about avant-garde directors, such as Sergei Eisenstein and Ingmar Bergman.

Cyril firmly believed that I could achieve anything I set out to do. I concluded early on that I would always have to be the main breadwinner in the family and although Cyril regretted this, he wasn't embarrassed. He encouraged my educational aspirations. I passed English and French A-levels through evening and correspondence courses while living in Bevin Court.

He taught me all I knew about literature and politics, as well as art and film, but in retrospect, I realize he was an eclectic educator. I doubt if anybody could have been more contrary in his opinions and interests.

Despite doing five hated years of military service as a gunner, he declared there was no finer nation than the Germans. While he abhorred the evils and insanity of Nazism, he admired the Germans' achievements in music, philosophy, art and literature.

He was never prejudiced against 'coloured' people, as we called them in those days, or homosexuality, which was illegal at the time. Such views were unusual for a British man of his age at that time. Even so, he hoped never to have a son as he couldn't bear the idea of him turning out to be 'queer'.

A communist in his youth, he firmly believed that 'workers must own the means of production', but hated wishy-washy British socialism, calling our 1960s Labour politicians wasteful and incompetent. He regarded women as being superior to men in most respects, especially emotionally. He idolized me but joked (and I think quietly meant it) that a woman's finest quality was obedience. He considered himself the absolute leader in our relationship.

LINSEED OIL AND
PALETTE KNIFE, 1966

Oil on canvas, 43 x 58cm (17 x 23in),
Collection Renske Mann

We're living in Walthamstow. Cyril
has taken the big bedroom in our
house to use as a paint room. We
sleep in the small bedroom at the
back. He has priority: after all, he
practically renovated our Victorian
cottage by himself. I work full time
to pay the mortgage. He gets busy
the minute I close the door. Metal
surfaces inspire him. Sunlight glints
on the tools of his trade and a
golden linseed oil bottle, casting
shadows against the wall.

Chapter 22

DARING AT LAST

Every picture was a fight. Nothing was ever good enough. When we met in 1959, Cyril had told me in despair that his paintings lacked daring. 'Too much emphasis on technique as a student is holding me back. If only I'd been self-taught, like Vincent, then I wouldn't care about painting badly or making mistakes. My art will always be grounded in realism, but my vision of light and shadow must be bolder and evolve into new dimensions.'

The year was 1963. I was twenty-four and considered myself grown up. For the past three years we had scraped by on my earnings. I worked three mornings a week at the Bahai Society of Great Britain, a spiritual/religious community of Persian origins, then as now based in posh Rutland Gate, Knightsbridge. Cyril, who disliked religions of any description, was not thrilled, but the job was easy and left me free to model and be with him on other days.

Occasional picture sales provided jam on our bread and butter. They were an important morale booster for Cyril: 'You can't pay me a greater compliment than putting your hand in your pocket,' he told his few admirers. 'Selling a picture is the ultimate proof of the pudding,' he concluded. Cheques would go straight into Cyril's bank account, but sometimes he was paid cash, which we could splash out on treats.

Nothing was ever planned. Time had no meaning for Cyril. He had never owned a watch and wasn't going to start now, just because I had become part of his life.

Cooking and housekeeping gradually became my job, causing a few spats. I was undisciplined and untidy. 'I must have order,' Cyril would scream at me. It was a good sign: in the past, during his nervous breakdown, everything was chaotic, a sure sign he couldn't cope. Now he needed to clear the decks before painting. I obeyed him immediately, piling up library books in a corner and shoving furniture aside, making space for his easel and canvas. Our living room, where we slept, ate and did everything else, was desperately overcrowded.

Cyril mostly painted in the morning. The minute he drew the curtains he knew when the weather was set to last. As the sun rose, it cast shadows from the Crittall windows across my nude body on our single bed. He stared at me, grunting and squinting. 'Stay put and take a comfortable pose,' he ordered. I knew by then that there was no such thing: every pose would turn into agony in time.

Until we met, Cyril nearly always painted from sketches. Financial constraints forced him to use paint frugally on a small second-hand canvas or board. He cursed himself for being too careful and not taking risks. He just couldn't let himself go.

'If you fancy painting a large canvas, then do it,' I urged him. We lived from hand to mouth, knowing that we could always get by on my secretarial jobs. He took me at my word, knocking up large stretchers covered with cheap hessian.

Tables and chairs had to be moved out of the way to make space for Cyril's easel. Shuffling between one tight spot and another, he never took his eyes off me. I stretched, yawned in the heat and put my hands under my head, twisting my torso at a slight angle from my hips.

It was midsummer. I tried to doze off. 'Concentrate, don't go to fucking sleep, chooky,' said Cyril. He was drunk with inspiration. He never stopped talking, explaining what he was doing and why, directly addressing his hero, Vincent. 'Before anything else, I must mass in the light areas first,' he said. 'Those are most important, not mid-tones or darks.'

Liberated at last, he painted at frantic speed to keep pace with the sun, rapidly moving around the room. He had to capture the dynamic effects of the rays bouncing off every surface, from walls on to my body and back. 'That's how to do it. I've been wrong all my life,' he gasped. What did he mean, I wondered? I didn't ask. I was sulking, not allowed to doze or move a muscle.

'Models at the RA haven't a clue', Cyril gabbled on angrily. 'They just sit on a chair. Students have to group around a podium. If you're in the wrong spot, you're fucked.' Then, as a back-handed compliment: 'At least you know how to make your body look interesting.' Perhaps, I thought bitterly, but my twisting torso is killing me. Please, please give me a rest.

I needed a loo break. He wouldn't hear of it. 'The sun is changing direction by the minute,' he growled. 'If you move now, it will be different in five minutes. Stay put, or I'll fucking kill you.'

Cradling the back of my head, my hands felt dead. My neck ached like hell. This was torment. 'If only you could be here all the time, modelling for me,' Cyril sighed, prodding away at his canvas. 'Then I could turn out some decent pictures.' God forbid, I thought.

'A painting often looks marvellous after the first few brush strokes,' he went on. 'Many artists leave it at that, looking slick, pretty and abstract, but that's cheating. I despair when I think I've taken a picture too far half-way. Then I must go on, all or nothing until it falls into place, or it doesn't. I can't put it right later. Painting direct without preliminary sketching is the most daring and difficult form of painting. That's how Vincent did it, too.'

Did I hear him say 'daring'? Yes, I did: thirty years after the Royal Academy Schools, Cyril had thrown caution to the wind. At last he was following in Vincent's footsteps. He dared!

Looking back almost sixty years, I sympathize with Paul Cezanne's unfortunate wife, Hortense Fiquet. He painted her forty-four times. I saw some of her portraits recently. Judged by her pained expression, she hated modelling as much as I did. It didn't help that she also grew to dislike her genius husband and vice versa.

Our relationship was still deeply unequal. Now in his early fifties and recovered from decades of ill health, Cyril was blessed with boundless energy. He was also self-obsessed and impatient with my inadequacies, never considering I was young and still had much to learn. He knew, though, that I wanted to help him fulfil his potential and create great paintings.

Cezanne had explored Hortense's image as he would have done an apple or still life. His unique interest was in the underlying structure of objects, which he wanted to render with a greater solidity than the Impressionists had done. Similarly, for Cyril my naked body was only a surface on which sunlight, rapidly drifting through our window, would bounce in constant movement.

He knew he could paint me as he wished, with the movement of light always taking precedence. He never needed to 'prettify' what he saw in order to flatter or please me.

We were introduced to Denis Norden, then a household name as a comedy writer and radio personality, by a mutual friend, Peter Davis. When they visited our flat, we prayed Denis would buy one of Cyril's paintings. He liked many and was particularly impressed by a painting showing sunlight streaming through our sitting room window and radiating in all directions from my naked body. Noting Cyril's passionate rendering of the light, Denis suggested that the painting should be called *Ecstasy*. Sadly, he didn't buy it, though when Peter suggested we give him the painting as it would be good for Cyril's reputation, the response was predictable: 'To hell with that,' Cyril replied.

As usual, when looking at this life-size reclining nude, it helps to half close your eyes as if staring into strong sunlight. You will then see the body's form emerging underneath the moving light. That's the meaning of *Ecstasy*.

ECSTASY, 1963

Oil on canvas, 61 x 91.5cm (24 x 35in), Private Collection

Cyril is beyond inspired: he's ecstatic as he opens the curtains in Bevin Court and sees my body's warm skin tones reflecting the bright sunlight. 'Stay where you are!' he orders, dragging in easel, canvas and paints He works rapidly and throws caution to the wind. 'It's taken thirty years to learn how to paint,' he grunts. 'What do you think, Renske?', he asks afterwards. 'It's beautiful. You've painted a masterpiece,' I answer. Sixty years later I still think so.

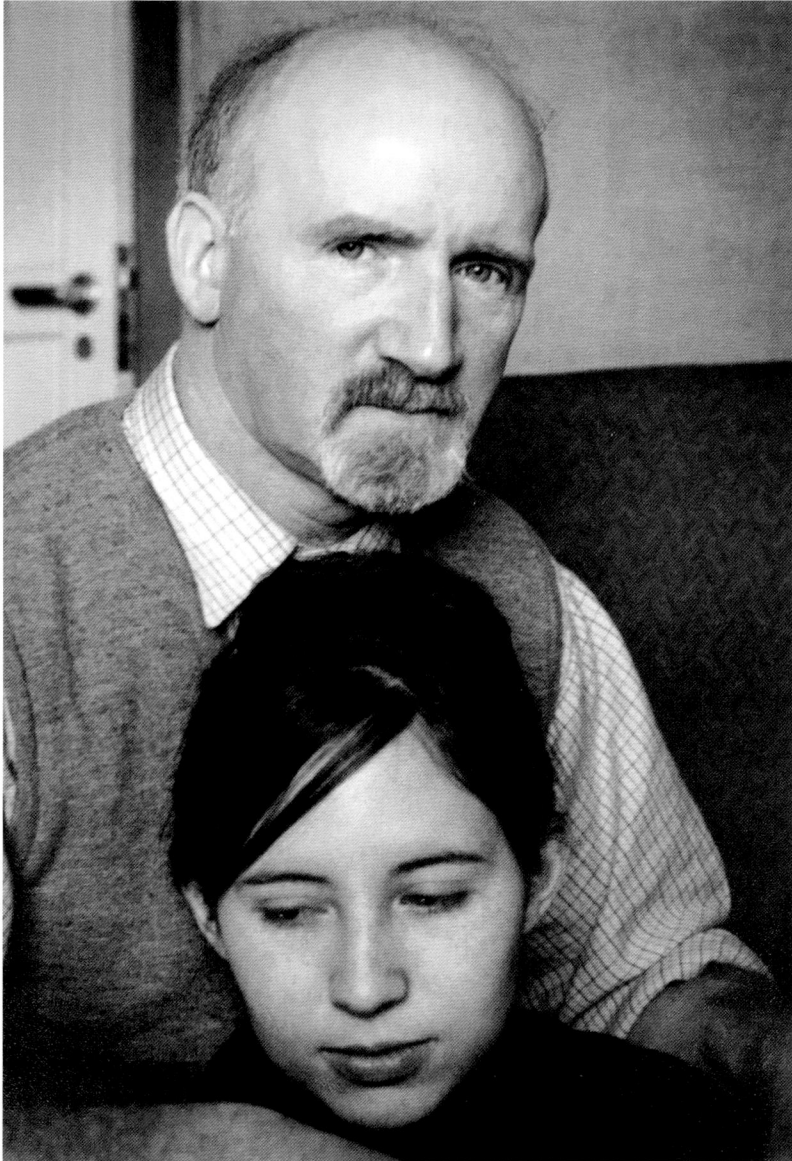

Those early years, in the 1960s, Cyril was my lover, teacher and father figure.
I promised to help him achieve his dream to become a great painter who would
revitalize figurative art, and persuaded him to give up teaching.

Chapter 23

A DAY AT THE SEASIDE

Our wants were minimal: neither of us drank alcohol. We didn't own a car, never went to a theatre, our clothes were cheap and drab with wear. Other than occasional family visits to Holland – my mother secretly paying our air fares unbeknown to my father or Cyril – we never went away on holiday.

Southend was where we liked spending Sundays. After a slow train ride from Liverpool Street, we'd walk from the station, stopping halfway to giggle at the dirty postcards. 'These are real art,' said Cyril admiringly.

'This is not real sea,' Cyril explained, spotting my disappointment. The tide was right out and would be for the rest of the day. I had my cozzie under my skirt. We took off our shoes, squelching through ankle-deep mudflats. I smelled fish and chips, malt vinegar and shellfish, but my first treat was candy floss on a stick.

'We'll take the little train down the pier,' Cyril proposed. 'It's the longest in the world, over a mile, and it would take too long to walk down. There's a sundeck at the end. No, you can't swim off the pier. Just watch the tide swirling around. It's dangerous.'

The threatening sky was gun-metal grey. It was chilly. We wrapped up in our coats and scarves, plonking ourselves down on acres of empty deck chairs when we thought nobody was looking. 'How much?' we asked the sullen attendant. He had turned up from nowhere. We scarpered without paying, as did everyone else in the crowd.

On birthdays, or whenever Cyril sold a picture, we treated ourselves. Our favourite meal out was at Maison Lyons Corner House in the Strand, where the all-you-can-eat, help yourself salad bar and pudding was a bargain.

Then came the first American-style grilled steak restaurants around Leicester Square. After Canada and travelling back to England via New York, Cyril knew all about these, but they were a new experience for me. Chargrilled, tough but tasty steaks came with a baked potato, dollop of sour cream and coleslaw. They were a step up from the ubiquitous Wimpy bars.

I tried but failed to persuade Cyril to take me for a Chinese meal. He flatly refused. Years ago in Vancouver's Chinatown he had chicken so chewy that he was convinced he was eating a seagull.

Chapter 24

A FRIEND IN NEED

Cyril was a steadfast and loyal friend, but in my early twenties, I tended to be unforgiving, especially when I felt let down, as was the case with a man we met at the Brush & Palette club. Charles came to visit us one evening, bringing his young, pretty girlfriend, and I found out he was in the carpet business. What luck: our living room needed re-carpeting after Cyril's nervous breakdown. I imagined a luxurious, fitted Wilton pile to set off our new red armchairs.

Cyril looked admiringly at the girlfriend and offered to paint her portrait. 'She's young and lovely,' he enthused. 'I'd do it now. If you wait ten years, she'll be past her best.' Charles was immediately interested when Cyril said he would accept a fitted carpet in exchange.

It was to be a highly finished, academic likeness, done over several sittings. The next day he bought a fine linen canvas and sable brushes. He posed the girl on a chair away from our window, avoiding sunlight and unflattering cast shadows. Sitting for hours and forbidden to chat, read or listen to music, his model was soon bored. Who could blame her? It didn't help that she was rapidly losing interest in her boyfriend.

As the painting progressed, Cyril refused to let her see it, worried that she might walk away if she didn't like it. He admitted to me that he was bored, too. The girl was beautiful, but her immature 'baby face' lacked character and did not inspire him.

After several posing sessions, Cyril finally agreed she could come and have a look. Had she any reservations, he asked? 'My nose is too long,' she replied. 'No problem. Take the pose again, and I'll adjust it and shorten it,' he promised. He continued painting for twenty minutes, then called her back for another look. 'Much better,' she said gratefully.

Cyril later confessed to me that he had not touched the model's nose in the picture. Any improvement was purely a figment of the girl's imagination. Charles was delighted with the end result, returning the next day with carpet samples. We picked a mid-grey shade that would be practical and not show every speck of dust.

Unfortunately, the girlfriend had dumped Charles, but this did not stop him from keeping his side of the bargain. His fitter arrived a few days later, when it was my turn to be disappointed.

Instead of a soft Wilton pile, Charles had fobbed us off with an inferior grade which looked suspiciously like ribbed sisal carpeting used in car interiors. Every bit of fluff and dust clung tenaciously, as it was clearly not wool and gave us electric shocks every time we touched our metal door handle or radiator.

Months later, Charles turned up one evening looking haunted and begging for a £100 loan. 'That's a fortune,' I whined. 'That fucking bloke is fly,' I hissed at Cyril. 'Shut up,' he reprimanded me. 'Don't use the word "bloke". It's common!' he said, ignoring my use of expletives.

Cyril disappeared and returned with twenty £1 notes raided from our joint savings. He handed the bundle to Charles, mumbling apologetically: 'It's all we can afford.'

Charles gratefully accepted the notes and fished a grubby handkerchief out of his pocket. Inside were what looked like bits of dull glass. 'They're uncut diamonds, worth far more than twenty quid. Keep them as security,' he urged. 'No, you keep them,' Cyril replied. 'I trust you.' I was convinced we'd never see Charles or our money again. He let us down with the carpet, so why should we believe him now?

We wrote off the outstanding loan after a few months. Then, in the middle of the night over a year later, I heard someone posting something through our letter box. It was an envelope with £20 with apologies from Charles for taking so long to settle his debt.

Cyril had helped him when he was desperate. He trusted him when few people would have done so. Not for the first time, he had proved to be a fine judge of character. 'If you lend money to a friend, you must be prepared to lose it,' he said at the time. It was another valuable lesson I learned from my husband.

Chapter 25

POLITICS

U nlike my husband, who 'knew everything', I was an ignoramus when it
came to politics. I wasn't interested and simply didn't care who ran the
country. That changed in 1961, when pictures of an alluring naked teenager
appeared on the front page of every newspaper. Christine Keeler's simultaneous
affairs with the Minister of War, John Profumo, and a Russian military attaché were
to bring down Harold Macmillan's Conservative government and have a dramatic
impact on social attitudes in Britain.

Cyril was thrilled by the images of Keeler sitting astride a dining chair and found
her incredibly sexy. He loved reading about the biggest scandal for generations and
for the first time I felt twinges of jealousy. Christine and her pal, Mandy Rice-Davies,
were not only sexually alluring but had a daring, devil-may-care attitude. Impressed,
I decided I had to be bolder to hold my husband's interest.

There was no question of me having an affair with a Minister of State,
but I got into politics in a different way, suggesting Cyril and I should go on a
demonstrationto be held in Trafalgar Square, where 70,000 people were expected
in support of the Campaign for Nuclear Disarmament (CND). Marching in protest
sounded so romantic and then there were those protest songs, all in a great cause:
unilateral nuclear disarmament. This surely was what Cyril believed in. Hadn't he
said: 'Russia won't shoot a sitting duck, will they?' In the event, however, he was
less than enthusiastic.

'Are you sure you want to go to the demonstration?' he asked. 'Are you ready for
the skirmishes? How would you feel about violence and if mounted police galloped
towards you? You could be arrested and jailed.' I was undeterred.

In the square I had never seen such a massive crowd. I was excited and felt part
of a great, idealistic moment. There was no space to sit anywhere and I quickly felt
tired. Then something strange happened: people began standing up, moving and
respectfully making way for Cyril and me to sit down.

Why this extraordinary show of respect? Young people had mistaken him for a
more famous artist who was expected to attend the CND meeting. With his beard
and long, unruly, straggly hair, Cyril resembled Augustus John and took advantage
of their supposed likeness. Unbeknown to the crowd, the renowned Welsh portrait
painter lay seriously ill in hospital. He died a few months later.

TRAFALGAR SQUARE, _c._1948

Oil on canvas, 56 x 46cm (22 x 18¼in), Private Collection

The sun slices through Nelson's Column in Trafalgar Square. Pigeons flutter in the polluted yellow sky. Down Whitehall stands the tower of Big Ben. This painting is exhibited but fails to sell in one of the world's top private galleries: Wildenstein's in New Bond Street. Cyril quarrels with the director. He's devastated. He can't provide for his wife, Mary, and daughter, Sylvia.

'It's not the first time people have mistaken me for Augustus John,' Cyril explained when we came home. 'I daren't walk around Chelsea, in case I'm punched by one of his illegitimate children. He's supposed to have over a hundred.'

Rudolph Dunbar was the first black man to conduct the London Philharmonic and Berlin Philharmonic orchestras in 1942 and 1945. When we meet at a party in 1960, he is the cultural attaché to the High Commission of Tanganyika. The territory is later renamed Tanzania when it gains independence from the United Kingdom.

Chapter 26

PARTY TIME

The 1960s were just about starting to swing when Cyril and I were invited to a smart party in Highgate given by a young 'power couple' who had bought some of Cyril's paintings: Peter Davis – an advisor to Harold Wilson – and his wife, Jean, who became a well-known children's radio broadcaster.

I dreaded going to parties with Cyril. For a decade, his stomach ulcers had kept him away from alcohol, but since his successful operation and recovery, he enjoyed hitting the bottle from time to time. And when he got drunk – which usually happened quickly – he could turn into a monster, insulting everyone who came his way and causing me agonizing embarrassment.

As we entered the room, Cyril introduced himself as 'the cradle snatcher', then left me to fend for myself among the crowd of Oxbridge-educated high-fliers and a sprinkling of celebrities. The mathematician Jacob Bronowski, later famous for his TV series *The Ascent of Man,* held court by the drinks table, while the University College London professor Douglas Wilkie and his doctor wife, June, told guests about their plans to cross the Atlantic to New York in their own sailing boat subsisting on a diet of the cat food Kit-e-Kat. Jack Mitchell, a music critic at the *Daily Mail*, mentioned that he had just received a demo from a new group called the Beatles, who he predicted would go far. The comedian Bob Monkhouse dropped in at one point.

Everyone seemed much older and more sophisticated than me. The only other person who didn't seem to know everyone in this glittering throng was a man sitting quietly in a corner, who introduced himself as Rudolph Dunbar. 'I'm a conductor,' he told me. As he was black, I assumed he must mean a bus conductor.

In fact, Rudolph was the first black man to conduct the London Philharmonic in 1942 and the Berlin Philharmonic in 1945. He was a clarinetist, composer and journalist who had achieved remarkable success conducting orchestras in the post-war years.

The mood of the party changed as everyone huddled round the black and white television set to hear Millicent Martin belting out 'That Was The Week That Was', introduced by the goofy-teethed David Frost. The satirical humour of the programme completely passed me by, as it did Rudolph.

I noticed Cyril scanning the room to find people to confront and prayed he had taken his medication. As usual, he was itching for a fight. 'What are you doing?'

I asked anxiously, trying to tear him away from a dangerous-looking encounter. 'I'm only trailing my coat, hoping somebody will step on it,' he replied with a wink. But Cyril managed to rein himself in when I introduced him to Rudolph, who was the very image of quiet dignity. He had just been appointed cultural attaché to the High Commission of Tanganyika, he told us, which seemed rather odd. But he asked if he could bring his boss – the High Commissioner – to meet us and see Cyril's paintings in Bevin Court.

A few weeks later, Rudolph duly arrived at our flat in a chauffeured black limousine, bringing with him not only the High Commissioner, but also one of the most mesmerizingly beautiful women I had ever seen, Princess Elizabeth of Toro. Princess of one of five traditional kingdoms of Uganda, Elizabeth – 'more royal than Princess Anne', Rudolph whispered to me – was a Cambridge graduate and the first East African woman to be admitted to the English Bar.

With her impossibly long, slender neck and serene brow, Elizabeth was already a fixture in the new colour supplements, though we of course hadn't heard of her. She asked a few questions about Cyril's paintings, but left most of the conversation to the two men – while I was overawed and kept quiet, as usual. At this moment she was in a relationship with the High Commissioner. Years later she had to flee Uganda after turning down a marriage proposal from Idi Amin.

The diplomatic party could not have behaved more graciously in our crowded little flat. There were no airs and graces, and Cyril, thank goodness, was on his best behaviour; though sadly our distinguished visitors didn't buy anything.

Chapter 27

THE GIRL IN THE GREEN JUMPER

By 1963, Cyril and I had lived together for three years. Many – I dare say most – people would have thought me a fool for throwing away my youth on a volatile, irascible and impoverished artist. But I had no regrets. Cyril's genius, inspiration and rich output in many bigger and more ambitious paintings were my reward.

I remember sitting one day in the red chair, with Cyril explaining why the green of my jumper looked so much more intense seen against the red upholstery of our G-plan suite. Suddenly he shouted, 'Don't you fucking move!'

He fetched his paint and brushes and completed my 'portrait' in less than three hours. The word portrait is in quotes, because it is not really a portrait, but again a painting of sunlight blazing on to me through the window, striking my face and bouncing all over the room. Even sixty years later, people comment that he has captured me body and soul. Yet had Cyril done a slicked-up, realistic version, it wouldn't have been as alive. My hands are a fingerless smear of paint. That, according to Cyril, was true abstraction, which literally means 'to leave out'. What people think of as abstract art is not actually abstract at all, but should be termed non-figurative, he insisted.

Supporting Cyril in his art was exciting, if not always enjoyable. Occasionally, I felt I was missing out. I wanted to get my youth back and swing along with the times. All work and little play was wearing me out and our Bevin Court flat sometimes felt like a prison.

The year 1963 became something of a watershed for us both. Cyril still relied on my earnings and never pretended otherwise. We were proud of our deep commitment to art. He dreamed of earning enough money so that I could stay at home and he could paint me all day. But I could think of nothing worse.

We were still deeply involved with art and each other, and so oblivious to the outside world we were unaware of the assassination of President Kennedy on 22 November 1963 in Dallas, Texas. With neither radio nor TV, and me still working part-time, we often didn't leave our flat for days. I remember our friend Dr Jack Bernfield dropping in, ashen-faced, lamenting, 'Isn't it terrible?'

'What's happened?' we asked, wondering what calamity had befallen him. He couldn't believe we didn't know about the assassination. We were living in a bubble that Cyril loved, but from which I occasionally longed to escape.

**DAFFODILS IN A
BRASS JUG (2), 1964**
Oil on canvas, 70 x 49.5cm
(27½ x 19½in), Collection
Piano Nobile, Robert Travers
(Works of Art) Ltd

Cyril's flower paintings
were not the chocolate-box
type. They were strong,
abstracted, glittering
renditions of colour and
light, beautiful, timeless and
intense.

LEFT RENSKE IN A GREEN JUMPER, 1963
Oil on canvas, 91.5 x 61cm (36 x 24in), Collection Renske Mann

I'm perched on the narrow wooden armrest of our red chair, which makes sitting still difficult
and painful. Posing requires concentration and willpower, but it doesn't stop me from
dreaming about our future.

Our food spending was minimal with Cyril still doing all the cooking. A fatty bacon knuckle provided our meals, floating in a pan of water in the kitchen that had a larder with an airbrick to keep food cool. Cyril carved the bacon and served it with lettuce (only the limp variety was available in those days), euphemistically calling it a ham salad.

Gradually the modelling sessions became rarer. I was now grown up and 'feeling my feet' – quite literally – encased in fashionable white Courrèges boots with holes at the top, showing off my legs, no longer in stockings but in sheer tights worn under pelmet-sized mini-skirts. I was making friends of my own and picking up good temporary jobs, including one for an advertising agency, Foot, Cone & Belding in Baker Street.

Now I started to think about what I could achieve for myself, other than being my husband's full-time model and muse. As I earned more with better jobs, I told Cyril we could afford to up his spending on paint and canvas. 'Paint bigger, use as much paint as you like,' I said. 'Forget your inhibitions, be bolder!' He took notice. While I was not there so often, modelling for him, Cyril would go to Chapel Street market to buy flowers as a substitute. 'They stay still and don't complain,' he said with a grim laugh.

Cyril was back, painting alone but with renewed confidence and creativity. Using bigger canvases and with no restrictions on the quantity of paint he used, he was enjoying himself – I convinced myself – even if he was on his own.

Back to mundane reality, before long the inevitable happened. I had a hole in my shoe and there was nothing left in the brown envelope. Not to worry, said Cyril, he would repair it. 'At least you will be able to wear the shoe until your next payday.' It so happened that he had been experimenting with linocuts, similar to woodcut but using domestic linoleum. He took a knife and scalpel and cut a piece to fit into my shoe.

Poverty felt raw and harsh. The welfare state was there, but no matter how bad things would get, Cyril would rather die than face the humiliation of signing on the dole. Anyway, he had deliberately made himself unemployed by giving up his teaching job, so it would have been hard if not impossible to qualify for benefits.

Economizing on food and clothes became second nature for us. Roaming around Chapel Street market, we bought mushroom stalks, never as expensive as whole mushrooms. We ate bacon offcuts and broken biscuits. When we still smoked, we scoured the streets for cigarette butts, plucking out unsmoked strands of tobacco to make rollups. By 1964, I had joined Cyril and given up smoking. We missed it dreadfully and sometimes I still do.

Chapter 28

LESSONS IN THE ART WORLD

I couldn't understand why the world in general, and the art world in particular, didn't appreciate Cyril's work as much as I did. If I was so astonished and exhilarated by the beauty of his paintings, why weren't others equally impressed? People, I concluded, just didn't understand what he was trying to achieve in his art. It was up to me to explain his vision.

This wasn't going to be an easy task, as I was soon to learn to my cost. The painting that convinced me of Cyril's genius when I first visited him in Bevin Court was *St Paul's from Moor Lane* – a painting that had been much admired at the 'Artists of Fame and Promise' exhibition at the Wildenstein Gallery in 1948, though it failed to find a buyer.

'Please, let me put it in for the Royal Academy Summer Show,' I begged him. He wouldn't hear of it. 'It's a racket,' he said. 'The better the painting, the less likely it will be accepted by the Academicians. Why? Because they don't want competition from outsiders who are better than they are. They make their living from what they sell at the Summer Show. They don't like outsiders, unless they're cronies.'

I refused to believe Cyril. 'How do you get a picture accepted then?' I asked.

'Impossible,' he continued. 'The RAs get ten times more applications than they have space to exhibit. They rake in the submission fees, paid by the mugs trying to get through. Anything that's good is rejected, but every amateur housewife's tiny effort will go on the wall.'

As a student at the Royal Academy Schools, Cyril had helped to do the fetching and carrying for the RA selection committee and seen the process in operation. 'Each picture gets about five seconds of consideration. Nobody has time to look for real quality,' he explained.

'Cunning bastards join the Chelsea Arts Club purely to smooch the RAs, buying them drinks and taking years to get pally. As friends, they get their pictures accepted. I wouldn't be seen dead, groveling like that.'

'Please, Cyril,' I pleaded. 'When they see a masterpiece like this, how can they fail to be impressed? They will be proud that you, an ex-RA student, can paint as beautifully as any old master.'

'Rubbish,' he replied. 'I've spent over twenty years trying to unlearn what they taught me at the RA Schools. I'd give my soul to paint as badly as Vincent. His

ST PAUL'S FROM MOOR LANE, 1948

Oil on canvas, 51 x 61cm (20 x 24in), Private Collection

Many successful artists gave London a wide berth after the war, but Cyril saw beauty in his bomb-ravaged environment. He recorded the damage, staring against the sun in a yellow sky with the dome of St Paul's silhouetted on the horizon. Unfortunately, few people wanted a reminder of the recent Blitz on their walls.

technique may be lacking, but his vision is uniquely passionate and original. As for me, I'm too aware of my technique. That's not good for an artist. With hindsight, I wish I'd stayed in Canada, like the Group of Seven, who were wonderful, natural painters and mostly self-taught.'

I decided to send off for the application forms, ignoring Cyril's objections. I was convinced that the selection committee would spot this masterwork and accept it. The expense of submitting a painting was a worry, but I felt it was an investment. There was a good chance of a sale at a premium price, should it be accepted.

Against his better judgement, Cyril let me go ahead. Unfortunately, he turned out to be right on every score. The painting was rejected, as he had predicted. I was heartbroken and disgusted. How could they? It was the first time I had felt something to equal Cyril's despair at his lack of recognition.

But I didn't stop trying to get the wider public interested in Cyril's work. He insisted he would never pay a gallery to show his pictures. That ruled out 90 per cent of all London establishments, who required not only 33 per cent commission, but also an up-front contribution to expenses, such as invitation cards, wine at the private view, postage and so on. Then there was the material cost of frames, canvases and paint.

St Paul's from Moor Lane is so subtle and atmospheric, I believe Turner and Constable would have been proud to have created it. It dates from the late 1940s, when Cyril painted facing the sun. London's iconic cathedral dome is silhouetted against a hazy, yellowish sky, dominating the surrounding buildings and bomb sites. A dusting of reflected light leads the eye into the composition, along a low brick wall. The sun glitters on the road surface, even picking out a round manhole cover. Men in raincoats and 1940s hats hurry to work, adding to the perspective and providing a sense of movement.

'Why the yellow sky?' I asked Cyril.

'It was when we had peasoupers,' he explained, 'fog and pollution caused by coal fires. That's what the skies really looked like.'

Some people wonder whether, at the bottom of his heart, Cyril didn't actually want to be recognized. It was true he could be his own worst enemy, and rarely bothered to make himself likeable. On the contrary, he often went out of his way to make enemies.

Cyril had Cezanne in mind when he did his portrait of David (overleaf). His alert features and slightly sceptical expression are rendered in impressionistic facets that seem to remain in flux. And Cyril was particularly proud of the way he painted the hands. Hands, he believed, should be as expressive in a painting as the face, and few artists, he boasted, including Picasso and the Expressionist Oskar Kokoschka, were as skilled at painting hands as he was.

David, however, disliked the portrait, refusing even to accept it as a gift. Perhaps it was just too truthful. 'Most people don't like their portraits,' Cyril grumbled. 'That's why I would never be a professional portrait painter. To satisfy your sitters, you must flatter them and make them look younger, which I simply refuse to do.'

The portrait languished in Cyril's stacks of unsold paintings for decades, until shortly before David's death I received a call from his daughters, wanting to buy the painting. I gave it to them in recognition of all their father and his wife, Hilda, had done for us. When the painting had been cleaned, restored and framed, David was finally reconciled to it, and felt pleased that his daughters and grandchildren had something to remember him by.

PORTRAIT OF DR DAVID HARDISTY, 1966
Oil on canvas, 76 x 51cm (30 x 24in), Private Collection

David Hardisty was a lawyer just starting his career as a patent agent when he fell madly in love with one of the most beautiful of Cyril's many paintings of sunlit flowers at the Rawinski Gallery in Newburgh Street. They had priced the painting at £300, which seemed a small fortune. David had recently married and simply couldn't afford it. He arrived at Bevin Court on his motorbike and strode up the staircase in his leathers, pleading with Cyril to accept £20 a month in fifteen instalments. We were happy to accept. Hardisty's passion for the painting seemed genuine, and the payments represented regular money. David proved to be the supporter of our dreams, going on to buy many more works over the years.

SKETCH FOR 'MANIFESTO PAINTING, LIGHT AND SHADOW', *c.*1950
Gouache on paper, 25.5 x 35.5cm (10 x 14in), Collection Renske Mann

Cyril rarely painted entirely from his imagination. One notable exception is his
manifesto painting, in which he visually explains the movement of light and shadow.
This gouache is one of several small versions before he completed his final oil painting,
using a symphony of greys.

Chapter 29

VISIONARY OR MADMAN?

'You know, Renske,' Cyril said to me one day, 'when William Blake had conversations with God and the angels, his wife used to join in.' It felt like a sad rebuke. Why wasn't I getting involved in his frequent spats with ol' Mike, ol' Vincent and Daddy Cezanne? He would say as much at times, looking dejected. But I was young, not well read and by now had little sympathy with Cyril's visions, which I was becoming convinced were closer to those of a madman than a visionary.

The diarist Henry Crabb Robinson, who knew the Blakes, wrote in 1852, some time after their deaths, 'His wife I saw at the time and she seemed to be the very woman to make him happy. She had been formed by him. Indeed otherwise she could not have lived with him. Notwithstanding her dress, which was poor and dirty, she had a good expression in her countenance, and, with a dark eye, remains of the beauty in her youth. She had the virtue of virtues in a wife, an implicit reverence of her husband. It is quite certain she believed in all his visions – in a word, she was formed on the Miltonic model and, like the first wife Eve, worshipped God in her husband. He being to her what God was to him.'

That passage made me weep when I read it years after Cyril died. Catherine Blake was five years younger than her husband, and illiterate when they met. She signed her marriage certificate with an X, and Blake taught her to read and write and also to engrave so she could become his assistant. She was his true helpmeet.

They had no children, unusual for the time, so Catherine could devote all her energies to her husband's career, which, like Cyril's, was uneven with many ups and downs. In those early days, I worshipped Cyril too, but as his wife I was simply not as spiritual and dedicated as Catherine had been to her husband. I loved Cyril's paintings, but I couldn't get involved in his conversations with his heroes, ol' Mike and Vincent, which were loud to the point of shouting due to his deafness. Cyril actually enjoyed these manic phases, but they were hell for the people who had to live with him.

In the early 1950s, he wrote in a notebook that he wanted to paint a symbolic picture of the curvature of the earth, with the sun rising above it, bursting light in all directions. Complementing his interest in the movement of light, the final composition included two Adam and Eve figures, casting their veil-like 'solid' shadows on earth. Entirely in grey-and-white tones, it is a biblical scene that combines all Cyril's theories on the movement of light and shape of shadows.

PORTRAIT OF SYLVIA AS A TODDLER, 1942

Oil on canvas, 50.5 x 40.5cm (19.9in x 15.9in), Private Collection

After three years at London's Royal Academy Schools, Cyril could have been a wealthy portrait painter, but rarely accepted commissions. 'I'm not prepared to flatter my sitters, which is what you must do if you want to be successful,' he told me. The few portraits he did are of his family, friends and himself. This one of his toddler daughter, Sylvia, shows the poor child close to tears. She recalled to her dying days the agony and boredom of sitting still for hours, clutching her doll.

Chapter 30

I WANT TO BE YOUNG

The girl in the green jumper was now getting ideas of her own. I was desperate for a radio and turntable, so I could listen to the kind of music that young people liked: Cliff Richard, the Beatles, Elvis, the Rolling Stones, Harry Belafonte and Dave Brubeck.

Cyril was scornful. 'Why do you want to listen to those long-haired lounge lizards?' he asked. Cyril's deafness made him sensitive to noise and he hated the idea of loud music blasting through our flat.

Yet he could sense trouble! I was unhappy. He knew that I must not be denied my daily bite of Freia's apple, which would keep me young and stop me longing to run away which, truth to tell, I had begun to consider.

At the time Camden Passage in Islington was full of pokey little shops including an electrical and radio outlet owned by a man who coincidentally was also called Cyril. When you passed by, this other Cyril and his wife could be seen at the back of the shop, tending to their precious little daughter, who had been born with a hole in the heart. The toddler was due to have a pioneering operation and everybody feared that she might not survive. When this Cyril heard that my Cyril was a painter, he offered him a deal: 'I'll swap you my baby's portrait for a Dansette.' The Dansette was at this time the record player that every young person wanted, including me.

Cyril returned next day with a camera to take pictures of the sick toddler. He painted her holding an orange, wearing a pale blue jacket, skilfully adjusting her unnatural complexion to make the little girl look like a normal, healthy child. Her parents were delighted with the result.

The next day after Cyril delivered his portrait, my dream came true. A bright red Dansette on spindly black legs arrived at Bevin Court. With my radio and turntable, I could now play music to my heart's content provided I didn't turn up the volume too much.

Sadly, the portrait of the girl that Cyril bartered in exchange for my treasured Dansette is now too damaged for reproduction. It was painted from photographs, because modelling for long periods would have been too great a strain for a sick child. We heard later that she survived the operation, although I have no idea if she made it to adulthood.

Cyril was extremely good at painting children but posing and sitting still is an ordeal for them. He painted his daughter, Sylvia, as a toddler. Clutching her dolly for comfort, her sad little face reveals her boredom and unhappiness at the experience, which she would remember for the rest of her life.

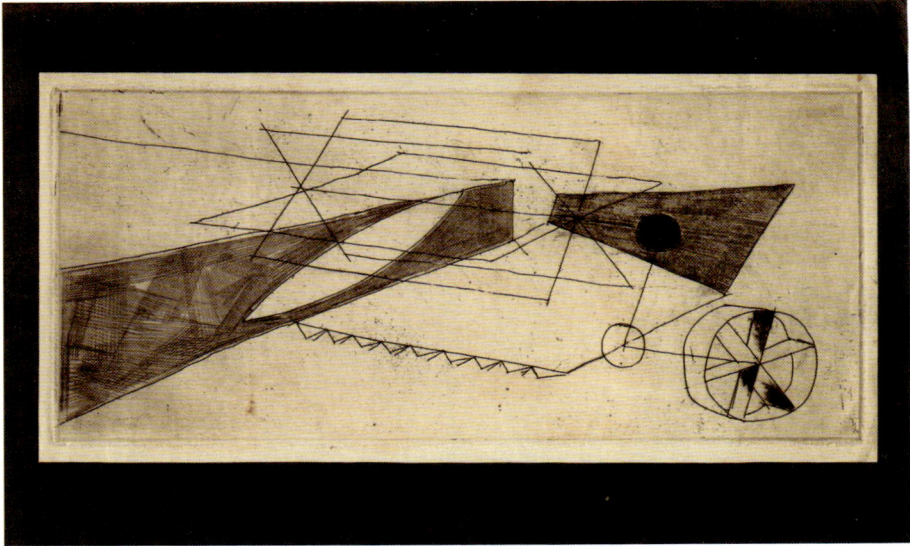

Best Wishes   from
Richard & Penny.

Cyril and Richard Hamilton had been friends since the war and worked on projects together. Richard attended Cyril's lectures on the technology of painting. I found two of his rare early etchings, used by Cyril as bookmarks, including this one, a Christmas card from Richard and his wife, Penny, to Cyril, which is in the Tate Gallery collection.

Chapter 31

CYRIL AND RICHARD

I n the 1950s, long before I came on the scene, Cyril had an almighty bust-up with a young artist called Richard Hamilton. You might think that Hamilton, the father of pop art, who famously declared that art should be 'sexy, gimmicky, glamorous and big business', and Cyril with his belief in timeless, painterly values wouldn't have had much to say to each other. However, long before the term pop art had even been thought of, they were extremely close for a time. But something had happened between them, and from the moment I heard about it, I was curious to find out more.

Hamilton at this point was already becoming well known – much to Cyril's disgust – and his response to my questioning was unequivocal. 'He's a fraud, a conman, an opportunist.'

'I thought he was your best friend,' I said. It was 1960, shortly after Cyril's nervous breakdown, and I had to tread carefully. Cyril had a sense of humour, but only on his terms.

'That fucker goes around brandishing a Balkan Sobranie pack, making people believe he's rich and famous,' he spat out with contempt. 'Typical of him. He keeps his roll-ups in the Sobranie pack.'

'That's hardly a hanging offence,' I laughed, as Cyril's face clouded over. He was paranoid and a bit of a hypocrite himself. On the rare occasions we went to a pub, he would fork out for a pint, but never manage to finish it. 'Why don't you just have a half?' I'd ask. Cyril would shrug sheepishly. 'It's unmanly to be seen with a half.'

It was clear that beneath these obfuscations there was more to Cyril's rupture with Hamilton than he cared to admit.

They had met in the late 1940s through a mutual friend, Pud Farmer, who had a business designing and building exhibition stands. While Pud did the designing, Cyril and Richard – who were both dexterous, practical and prepared to turn their hands to anything – joined forces in constructing and installing the stands. In job applications of the period, Cyril described this work as 'model making'.

At this point, Cyril was the better known of the two, already a respected figurative painter with several West End shows under his belt and an admired teacher, lecturing on the technology of painting at the Sir John Cass College. Several ex-Royal Academy students, including Cyril's then girlfriend, Audrey Whitfield, and indeed Richard himself, would come there to sit at his feet.

Richard, a decade younger, hailed from a similar working-class background: a car-showroom driver's son, he'd left school without qualifications, studied at various art colleges, and had just completed National Service when he met Cyril. He was a friendly young man and very open – certainly at this stage – to everything Cyril had to offer. For many years, Cyril and Richard socialized, supported each other and worked together, though they never, as far as I know, collaborated on any art projects. And from what Cyril told me, this was just as well. He and Richard were clearly destined to clash sooner or later. Their talents and artistic aims were so different.

Richard's gift was to pick up on new ideas and trends from Europe and, particularly, America, and feed them into the then narrow and parochial conservative British art scene, while putting his distinctive spin on them. He'd turn his hand to forms his older friend instinctively despised, such as collage – now a mainstay of all art education, but then almost breathtakingly obscure.

Taking paper cuttings and gluing them on to an oil painting wasn't proper art, as far as Cyril was concerned. He also dismissed the literary and – he believed – gimmicky contents of Richard's collages, one of which, *Just what is it that makes today's homes so different, so appealing* from 1956, made him famous. This initially notorious, now iconic picture showing a satirized aspirational interior is comprised largely of images lifted from American magazines.

'An artist's vision is all that matters: subject matter is irrelevant,' Cyril explained. 'There's only one criterion: does the painter make us see nature in a new way? Literature is the realm of the writer: nobody would admire Rembrandt today on account of the way he interpreted biblical scenes. He's celebrated forever because he showed people a new way of seeing light and shadow.'

ABOVE
Through our friends and sponsors, Dr Michael Leibson and his sculptor wife Sylvia, we met Islington photographer Edward Hutton, who took this photograph of Cyril in 1960.

The two men's temperaments were entirely different. Cyril was irascible, awkward, volatile, but saw himself as incorruptible in art, which he was convinced must be timeless. He believed that it was a vocation. He loathed gimmicks.

Richard, on the other hand, was likeable and sociable, with an instinct for moving in the right circles, and receptive – in all senses – to everything happening around him, including Pud Farmer's exhibition designs; a matter I heard about from Pud himself.

Pud and Irene, his partner, lived on the top floor of a handsome Georgian house in Fitzroy Square, filled with budgerigars that swarmed in and out through the open windows. They were famous for their noisy, boozy parties. But by the time Cyril introduced me to them in 1960, the parties were over. The bohemian couple were then nearing retirement age. One day I learned that they had also fallen out with Richard. 'That bastard stole my designs and calls that art!' thundered Pud.

In 1955 Richard organized an exhibition called 'Man, Machine and Motion' at the ICA comprising photographic images of man in 'aquatic, terrestrial, aerial and interplanetary' motion, clipped in dynamic arrangements to portable steel modular frames, with some panels left blank for the viewer to 'generate their own compositions'. It is now regarded as one of the defining exhibitions of its time, an early example of installation art and an attempt to conceive of an exhibition as a work of art in its own right. As far as Pud was concerned, however, Richard had simply purloined his display techniques without credit, never mind financial remuneration.

A second Hamilton installation, 'An Exhibit', created with Victor Pasmore in 1957, went even further in turning the sort of exhibition design methods on which Richard had worked with Cyril into art, featuring coloured Perspex sheets hanging from wires in an interactive arrangement that allowed an infinite number of possible variations.

As abstraction became the dominant force in European and American art throughout the 1950s, to be superseded by pop art towards the end of the decade, Cyril doggedly stuck to his ideal of taking nature as his point of departure, quietly exploring the dynamic and transformative effects of sunlight and shadow for over half a century. He saw himself as the true successor to Rembrandt, Turner, the Impressionists and all other artists of the past who, like him, had rendered light in a new way.

He condemned Jackson Polleck's Abstract Expressionism, refusing to accept that 'future art would be restricted to decorative, accidental blobs of paint, where the painter's sole function is to know when to stop.'

Richard meanwhile had already moved beyond abstraction, declaring in 1957 that 'Pop Art is transient, expendable, low-cost, mass-produced, young, witty, sexy.' By that time he and Cyril had already cut off all contact and I was never able to get Cyril to tell me precisely what had happened.

Cyril and Pud Farmer wrote Richard off as a fraud, but perhaps he was just an artist of his time, the age of the ready-made, when appropriating whatever is around them is simply what the artist does. Cyril, meanwhile, stuck doggedly to his artistic principles in which honesty was the only true yardstick. 'Some paintings have broken every law of good design, but still finished as a work of art. Perhaps the one necessity, but the rarest thing in art today, is honesty.' Cyril held unwaveringly to his beliefs. But while he was resigned to his lack of recognition, it embittered him and finally drove him insane.

SELF-PORTRAIT WITH PAINTBRUSH, 1966
Oil on canvas, 71 x 56cm (28 x 22in), Collection Renske Mann

Cyril wrongly believed that he owed his fine perception of colour to his violet-blue eyes. However, colour is sensed in the cones in the retina at the back of the eye and not in the iris.

Chapter 32

A BRUSH WITH FAME

Although he often felt unappreciated, Cyril had several encounters with fame and certainly had his admirers – loyal buyers who believed in him, the Leibsons being prime examples. But they were occasional spikes rather than continuous accolades, rather like an actor who, although brilliant, only gets occasional parts.

Just before we moved out of Bevin Court, I had responded to an advertisement from a new gallery inviting submissions from artists for future exhibitions. The gallery was to be in a large and prominent Mayfair location. Cyril bundled up some paintings and I took them to show to the owners, two charming young men, Denys Alwin Davis and his partner, Ronald Dongworth. As soon as I untied the paintings, Ronald was overcome. 'Here's the artist for our opening show,' he said.

Denys and Ronald asked Cyril to provide fifty works for their inaugural show, with the choice left to him: the biggest body of Cyril's paintings to be seen by the public to date. The Alwin Gallery, at 56 Brook Street, faced Claridge's and was to become one of the biggest and most ambitious commercial galleries in Europe.

Denys Davis – a former couturier and 20th Century Fox cameraman, who had been a British judge at the Cannes Film Festival – had designed the interior, based on his experience of lighting films. Ninety profile projectors, each of which had four shutters, could be adjusted to provide tailor-made lighting for each picture. Cyril was instructed to supply his paintings in black strip frames that would blend into the walls, also painted black.

Cyril was horrified at this and simply refused. I begged him to keep quiet and not air his opinions, but he was intransigent. The best way to show paintings, particularly his paintings, was in the closest approximation of daylight: fierce spotlights would flatten the impasto on his pictures, making them appear like transparencies projected against the black walls.

I had to keep Cyril away from Ronald and Denys. It was their project, they paid the bills and they had the right to follow their own ideas. It would have been open warfare if I hadn't stopped Cyril complaining, and he would have lost this fantastic chance to show his work.

It wasn't just the gallery that had to look wonderful. The artist's wife had to have a makeover as well. Ronald and Denys decided that I needed sprucing up for the private view and had a long silk evening dress made for me, also paying for a professional make-up artist and hairdressing session. I felt unrecognizably elegant. Cyril wore the Austin Reed suit we had bought earlier, looking smart and every bit the successful artist.

The gallery looked amazing with its unique lighting system. Newspapers remarked on it, paying it more attention than the art, though the crowds at the celebrity-studded private view were more appreciative. The dramatist Arnold Wesker, author of the 1962 hit play *Chips with Everything*, was there, as was Dr John Robinson, Bishop of Woolwich, author of the controversial bestseller *Honest to God*, who bought a large flower painting.

Several pictures sold to American buyers and total sales exceeded £1,000, as much as I earned in a year at the time, though it wasn't quite the massive change in our fortunes we had been hoping for. However, Denys and Ronald hadn't yet built a clientele and were largely reliant on guests from Claridge's to wander across to the gallery.

One large Bevin Court interior had sold to a young executive named Avril Taylor, who asked us to accept payment in instalments, which we were happy to do. A few months later she mentioned that she could have sold her picture for a lot more than she had paid for it. I assumed she was trying to be kind and didn't pay much attention.

Years later, however, I learned that another visitor had also set his heart on that Bevin Court interior and had asked to be put in touch with the buyer. Avril had been called by a male secretary, saying his employer was prepared to offer twice as much as she had paid for the painting. When Avril refused, the secretary rang again, offering three times as much. Still Avril refused. When the offer went up to four times what she'd paid, Avril told the secretary, 'I don't care what your boss is prepared to pay. I'm keeping the picture. I love it.'

This buyer, Avril revealed to me, was Paul Getty, then the richest man in the world. In retrospect, it was sad for us. It would have been a tremendous accolade to have Cyril's work – a painting of an impoverished council flat in Islington indeed – included in one of the greatest art collections in the world, housed in two museums in California. Still, I don't doubt that Avril got a great deal of pleasure from the painting.

SUNLIT ROSES, 1966
Oil on canvas, 91 x 59.7cm (35⅞ x 23½in), Collection Renske Mann
It helps to see paintings like this, the way Cyril sees the roses in a green glass vase.
Half-squeeze your eyes to focus against the dazzling light, and everything falls into place.

Chapter 33

NEW FRIENDS

Cyril rarely spent time with fellow artists. He despised the notion of joining a group or collaborating with others in evolving a style. 'Fuck Surrealism, Cubism or Minimalism', he said. 'No artist worth his salt would ever want to follow an ism'. He was proud to plough his own, lonely furrow for almost half a century, refusing to visit exhibitions, certainly by living artists, at the Tate or in commercial galleries.

There was a serious downside to his isolation: he came to rely on me as the sole judge and jury of his work. I felt I wasn't up to it. I was only in my early twenties, my art knowledge was limited and my eye was still untrained. Paradoxically, the more I learned about art and what Cyril aimed to achieve, the harder I found it to give him what he craved: an instant assessment. Left alone all day, he couldn't wait for me to come home from work, spotting me through the window as I walked down the path to Bevin Court.

When a foul whiff of turps and oils met me as I opened the door, my heart sank. The light must have been good, and he'd been painting! He would turn around his easel so I could focus fully on his new picture. 'Give me your honest opinion, no bullshit,' he would beg. He breathed down my neck, eyes blazing. Was the painting any good or should he scrape it off? He stared at me, aching for a response. He reeked of sweat and exhaustion, euphoric one moment, insulting the next.

When this happened, I would struggle for words. I desperately needed time to absorb his new creation, while he hovered over me anxiously. Some canvases screamed 'masterpiece', but others were harder to assess on the spot and required contemplation. My silence drove him to fury. Then anger and disappointment would turn into self-pity. He accused me of being uncaring and selfish, of thinking only of myself and losing interest in his art. Noting the heavy impasto on a canvas, I timidly asked if he'd used a palette knife. 'I'm a painter, not a fucking cook,' came his withering reply.

One day he was so angry that he chucked his paint-laden palette at the easel. While it was not aimed at me, I ducked instinctively as it landed face down on the recently acquired carpet. 'Oh no,' Cyril howled. He quickly came to his senses, seeing the damage. 'Not fucking Prussian Blue again,' he swore. The mess on the floor was distressing as he had recently painted a woman's portrait and bartered it for our new carpet.

PORTRAIT OF CYRIL, 1975
Monoprint by Zsuzsi Roboz

The Hungarian artist Zsuzsi Roboz asked Cyril to pose for her in 1975. Both attended evening classes in printmaking at the Sir John Cass College in East London. Her perception of her friend and mentor as a gentle old man made me see Cyril in a different light. Zsuzsi presented the portrait to me shortly after he died.

Cyril always took steps to protect the carpet, spreading overlapping dust sheets around his easel before he started working. Unfortunately, he shuffled and danced, moving back and forth like a boxer, jabbing at his canvas with brushes held at maximum arm's length. Gaps would appear between the dust sheets, but Cyril was too preoccupied to notice. He dragged his easel around the room, chasing the sun as it sped through the window. Increasingly emotional as he ran out of time, he swore at his canvas: 'Do as you're told, you fuckpig.'

When he saw the paint spill, he sank to his knees to clean up the damage. Sod's law, he groaned. Prussian Blue was his bête noire. No matter how thoroughly he covered up, blobs of paint escaped from his brushes, leaving indelible stains on our carpet and furniture.

If only Cyril could find a friend who was involved in art and understood what he was going through, it would make my life so much easier. I began to loathe his neediness, his pathetic demands for praise and reassurance. I hoped that a good artist friend could occasionally take some of the pressure off me. That was exactly what happened.

Simon Hieger, an elderly portrait painter then in his nineties, invited Cyril to exhibit with the Contemporary Portrait Society, which he had founded with an inaugural exhibition at the Wildenstein Gallery in Bond Street in 1961.

MANN '72.

STUDIO CORNER, 1972

Oil on canvas, 80 x 100cm (31 x 39in), The Estate of Cyril Mann / courtesy of Piano Nobile, Robert Travers (Works of Art) Ltd

This large composition of jugs, jars and brushes in Cyril's paint room has some of the formalized elements of his 1950s 'solid-shadow' paintings. Using line, he now works in natural daylight. The shadows are cast by sunlight and not, as before, by an electric lightbulb. His palette in the foreground leads the eye in.

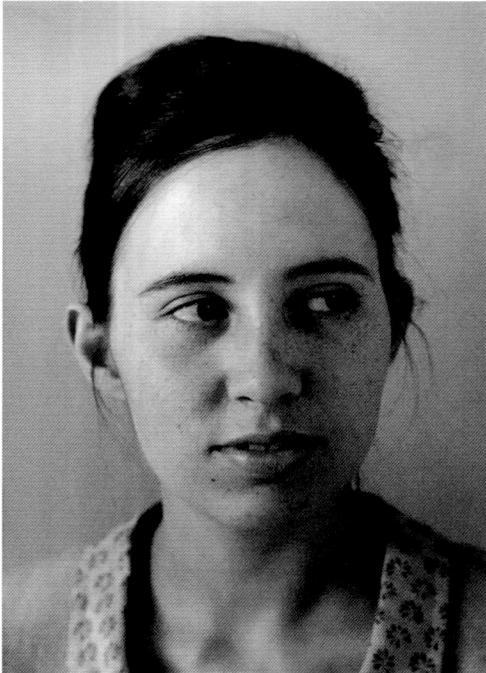

Growing up and climbing the career ladder in 1967, as a trainee PR executive.

Portrait painting was in danger then of becoming a moribund art form, a situation Hieger blamed on the Royal Society of Portrait Painters, which dominated official portrait commissions, stifling innovation and encouraging its members to paint in an academic, realistic style that pleased the wealthy conservative establishment.

Cyril strongly agreed with his new friend. Portraiture, as Hieger wrote himself in a catalogue introduction, should serve 'as a bridge between ageless art and the art of our age'. While Cyril had missed the society's first Wildenstein show, he was pleased to take part in several later exhibitions. He joined the Contemporary Portrait Society's (CPS) selection committee in 1965, when fellow members included R. O. Dunlop, Peter Greenham and Hans Schwartz. The committee agreed that the priority should be to attract the best and most creative painters and sculptors of their day.

Shows took place at major West End Galleries, including the Upper Grosvenor Gallery, which offered the society a permanent centre on its premises. Excellent reviews helped to attract major talent, such as Ruskin Spear, Kyffin Williams and Joseph Herman.

'It's a shame that portrait painting is unpopular with young artists,' Cyril said during a committee meeting. 'They lack the right skills, as learning to draw is no longer obligatory in art schools.' He suggested that the CPS should sponsor an award scheme aimed at encouraging young artists and students. The committee agreed and began to cast around for venues and sponsors. While these efforts foundered, years later – after Cyril and Simon Hieger had died – the National Portrait Gallery introduced its own annual portrait award for artists under thirty, which runs to this day.

Cyril made no particular friends on the committee until he found an unlikely kindred spirit in a striking young Hungarian woman called Zsuzsi Roboz, who invited him to see her work at her Pimlico studio. Cyril was impressed, particularly by Zsuzsi's drawings of girls working in the Windmill Theatre. She had been invited by Sheila van Damm, the theatre's owner, to capture its 'last days backstage'.

Cyril advised Zsuzsi to learn lithography and turn these historic pictures into small editions. And he suggested they take lithography evening classes together at the Sir John Cass College in Moorgate, where, a decade earlier, he had lectured on the technology of painting. Now he would be joining Zsuzsi as a student.

He was taken aback when she arrived for the first lesson in a chauffeur-driven Rolls Royce. Zsuzsi and Teddy Smith, her adoring, rich and supportive husband, lived in a palatial apartment in Bryanston Court, Marble Arch, the very one in which the Prince of Wales, later King Edward VIII, had first consorted with the American divorcée Wallis Simpson before the war. Their valuable art collection included oils by van Gogh, Monet and Modigliani, to which they soon added some of Cyril's paintings and drawings. Cyril, in turn, thought Zsuzsi's Windmill lithographs were so accomplished, he recommended she contact the Theatre Museum, which was then a part of the Victoria & Albert Museum. It was a good move: the curators bought an edition for their permanent collection.

Zsuzsi later drew a wonderfully sensitive portrait of Cyril, which gave me a very different perspective on my husband: to her he wasn't a frightening, bullying ogre, but a sweet, wistful and melancholic old man nearing the end of his life.

I contributed to the CPS in my own way, volunteering as honorary secretary and serving under its chairman, Carel Weight, Professor of Painting at the Royal College of Art. I was a good organizer with rapidly developing PR skills, and I soon made myself indispensable. Before long, members were asking me to write their press releases.

Through the society I met and corresponded with many distinguished artists. Despite his great age, Duncan Grant, the Bloomsbury Group survivor, would travel all the way from Charleston to submit his portrait for an exhibition. The Expressionist illustrator Feliks Topolski entered a portrait of Prince Philip. One year a very elderly Dame Laura Knight walked into a private view, leaning heavily on a stick. I had met art world royalty, I was told.

Chapter 34

WHAT A DIFFERENCE A YEAR MADE

After four years of living in Bevin Court's cramped conditions, I desperately wanted to move to a proper house of our own. With help from Cyril's early benefactor Erica Marx and the utmost frugality on our part, we saved enough for a deposit on a small house in Walthamstow. This was far out in East London, where no fashionable artist would be seen dead, but handy for us as it would be near the soon-to-be-built Victoria Line into central London. Erica Marx had always promised to leave some money to Cyril and reckoned she might as well do it now, when our need was greatest.

Our house, 97 Lynmouth Road, E17, cost £2,700, and was in terrible condition. It took two years to make it habitable. It required a large £700 deposit. It was an awful problem securing the mortgage because a wife's income counted for little in those days.

Cyril, however, had started making good picture sales and had a record of employment as a part-time teacher until recently. We had always paid our council rent on time, Cyril over many years before we met. Paying for two places at once while our Walthamstow house was modernized and made habitable was a huge struggle. It meant I had to take a full-time job, so we could manage both Bevin Court's rent and our mortgage simultaneously.

In those days, councils offered grants for modernizing houses: installing a bathroom, indoor toilets, hot-and-cold running water, and towards a kitchen with a larder – though still no fridge. The maximum grant would have been £300, a useful sum, around £7000 today. Unfortunately, we were only eligible for half the amount.

Cyril and Tom – an ex student of Cyril's who became a plumber – would leave first thing most mornings, taking the train from Liverpool Street. Cyril helped Tom do the labouring, digging a deep inspection chamber in the garden, as specified by the council. By now he had recovered well from his operation and was stronger and fitter than he had been for many years.

He and Tom plumbed in a brilliant canary-yellow bathroom suite, which seemed the height of chic in 1965. He laid rustic quarry tiles in the kitchen and built the units himself. He wallpapered every room and constructed a larder with an airbrick on the outside wall. Like his builder father and grandfather before him, and in common with many artists, Cyril was a highly efficient handyman. He could turn his hand to anything, from carpentry to bricklaying and decorating.

After years in a high-rise block, it was lovely to step out of the back door into our little garden with its apple tree and raspberry canes. The street itself was slummy, but after living in one room, we finally had a separate bedroom.

In saying goodbye to Bevin Court, I had taken over the reins. I had finished my year of temping at the advertising agency in their PR department, and was now an assistant with a proper, permanent job. This, I realized, was where I wanted to be, not a secretary-cum-dogsbody but an executive, creative in my own right.

As we closed the door for the last time on our Bevin Court flat, Cyril wept. 'I'm holding you back,' he cried. He was now as besotted with me as I had been with him in the early days.

As our relationship progressed, I became giddy with self-belief thanks to Cyril's constant and genuine encouragement. He had convinced himself – and me – that I could achieve anything I put my mind to. 'Nobody understands art and artists like you do. You should write about it,' he urged.

Cyril was an early 'house husband', always providing meals on the table when I came home from work. He never tried to hide our financial situation and our respective roles, but still dreamed of the day when he could earn enough to live on his paintings with me constantly by his side.

His belief in me drove me on to succeed in my career. I revelled in the new self-confidence that I owed largely to him. Like Blake and his wife, Catherine, he had 'shaped me' over the years.

'You could become a good copywriter yourself,' one of the agency directors told me. It was true: I had discovered a talent. I could write! In English! On my Olivetti portable I tapped out articles for art magazines, for which I was commissioned and even paid.

By this time, I'm glad to say, I had made peace with my parents, who had come to respect Cyril. My brother Bas and his wife Jose appeared to like him as well. They had even bought some of Cyril's paintings, not just to help us out, but because they actually admired them. My parents never made it to Bevin Court, but they did come to London after our daughter, Amanda, was born in 1968, after which Cyril and I travelled to Holland almost every year. He painted many pictures of Dordrecht's old city centre, which looked like a miniature Amsterdam, and of the pretty environs of my parental home.

RAILWAY BRIDGE OVER THE CULVERT, WALTHAMSTOW, *c.1967*
Oil on canvas, 46 x 58.5cm (18¼ x 23in),
Private Collection

When we moved to Walthamstow, Cyril never expected to find so much inspiration on his doorstep. The culvert under the railway bridge features in many paintings. The tranquil stream reflects the blue sky. The structural elements of this painting remind me of Cezanne's landscapes.

WALTHAMSTOW MOON RISE, 1968
Oil on canvas, 68.5 x 81cm (27 x 32in), The Estate of
Cyril Mann / courtesy of Piano Nobile, Robert Travers
(Works of Art) Ltd

It's night-time in 1968. The moon rises as Cyril roams
the streets, distraught and worried. Painting helps
to occupy his anxious mind and make him feel less
lonely and insecure. I'm in Thorpe Combe Maternity
Hospital with high blood pressure, awaiting the birth
of our baby. A man walks his dog past a wooden gate
towards a parked car.

Chapter 35

INSPIRATION IN WALTHAMSTOW

We had not expected to find beauty on our doorstep in Walthamstow. Traipsing around the allotments, Cyril found people wrapping prized dahlias in white paper bags to protect their blooms from wind and rain. Going out in all weathers, he would kick off his muddy shoes in the hall before going upstairs to his own paint room. For the first time, he had a perfect space to work, without getting in anybody's way or having to shift furniture.

He squared up his drawings and small oil sketches on large canvases. This is when he also began to experiment with acrylic paint, still relatively new on the art market.

There were no other artists in our street, Lynmouth Road, but to our delight and surprise, Cyril quickly made friends and felt at ease. He wandered down Walthamstow market, picking up curious new vegetables to paint, such as aubergines and red peppers, which he'd only ever seen in Ibiza but never here.

Walthamstow, and later Leyton where we moved after Amanda was born, was changing before our eyes: huge tower blocks rose, dwarfing the small semi-derelict Victorian cottages in their shadow. In the distance was Walthamstow's own power station, which locals considered an eyesore. Brick chimneys and massive wooden cooling towers dominated the skyline.

Cyril was inspired: he roamed around day and night, observing passing trains and noting in drawings and numerous paintings the changing vibes of the area. Then, when he'd had enough, he would explore the upcoming middle-class areas of Walthamstow Village, centred around the ancient St Mary's Church, where William Morris, founder of the Arts and Crafts Movement, had been baptized. Samuel Pepys also attended services there. On bright days, sunlight bounces off the church tower through trees and gravestones. Cyril would be there, sketching and painting, to his heart's content.

The first time Cyril took our baby in her tiny second-hand pram down to the market, the stall holders were enchanted. They ruffled her little head as Cyril passed

WALTHAMSTOW ALLOTMENTS, 1972
Oil on canvas, 87.5 x 112cm (34$^1/_2$ x 44in),
William Morris Museum, Walthamstow

Traipsing around allotments near Lynmouth Road in
Walthamstow gave Cyril peace of mind. In his final
years he was a keen gardener himself, growing all our
own fruit and veg in our garden.

along, shopping and chatting. We were a local curiosity as a couple: they were in awe of his talent and were curious about me, being so much younger, especially when he boasted that I was the breadwinner in our family. I had already gone back to work. There was no maternity leave in those days!

When he came home later, he was in for a big surprise. As he lifted the baby out of her pram, he found a hoard of silver coins quietly shoved under her blankets by the stall holders. It was lucky, they said, 'to touch a baby's head with silver'. Cyril was moved to tears.

When we had moved to Leyton a couple of miles down the road, we took our toddler daughter on the bus down Lea Bridge Road, across Hackney Marshes. There was a pub on the river. From the terrace deck we could see a Metropolitan Water Board pumping station. Half a century later, Amanda still remembers dangling a net in the water, fishing for minnows with daddy by her side. We took the minnows home in a jam jar to put in our garden pond, which was full of frogs already.

Cyril with his painting *The Flood Relief Canal*, 1967.

GAS COOLING TOWERS, WALTHAMSTOW, 1967

Oil on canvas, 44 x 57cm (17¼ x 22¼in), The Estate of Cyril Mann / courtesy of Piano Nobile, Robert Travers (Works of Art) Ltd

Cyril was fascinated by the massive wooden gas cooling towers, which dominated the modern skyline until 1969, when they were demolished to make way for the last Tube station on the new Victoria Line. Like Monet painting Rouen Cathedral, he would go out in all weathers to capture the giant industrial icon which generated local electricity supply.

Drawing of a woman with
a pram walking under the
railway bridge, around the
corner from our Victorian
cottage in Walthamstow.

WALTHAMSTOW GAS COOLING TOWERS AT NIGHT, 1968
Oil on canvas, 80.5 x 109cm (31³/₄ x 43in), The Estate of Cyril Mann / courtesy of Piano
Nobile, Robert Travers (Works of Art) Ltd

Painted at night, a train approaches, its lit windows streaking past as a man walks
along the wire fence. Workers report for their night shifts in the bright light of the
open entrance. The dazzle reflects in the night sky and ghostly tree branches.
A lone car is parked by the side of the road.

LORD OF THE FLIES or **PIG'S HEAD AND BEEF BONE, 1966**
Oil on canvas, 48 x 73cm (18³/₄ x 28³/₄in), The Estate of Cyril Mann / courtesy of Piano Nobile,
Robert Travers (Works of Art) Ltd

As a near-vegetarian, I often look back in horror at what we ate in the 1960s and '70s.
Cyril found an unusual admirer in Bill Jones, our local butcher, who supplied him with offal,
including this pig's head. He painted several versions, including one that Bill bought to
hang in his shop.

Chapter 36

GHOULISH TASTE

C yril had a ghoulish streak, a taste for blood and guts he shared with many great artists including Rembrandt, Chaim Soutine, George Stubbs and Francis Bacon, whom he admired precisely for the sexual and sadistic cruelty of his imagery. He made friends with our local butcher, Bill Jones in St James Street, who would give Cyril his offal: pigs' heads, beef bones; eviscerated hares and boiling fowls made good subjects.

Cows' lungs, known as 'lights' and used as pet food, hung and stank in his paint room. Like Stubbs, who left a flayed racehorse rotting in his studio while he did his anatomical drawings, Cyril would work on rotting animal parts until I could no longer abide the smell of death and decay.

Cyril had always been ghoulish. When Mary, his first wife, suffered a miscarriage, he swiftly painted a *Portrait of my Son*, showing a bloody foetus in a chamber pot. His crass insensitivity, as Mary saw it, led to their separation. Mary was understandably devastated. I fear that Cyril was relieved: he, Mary and Sylvia were barely coping as it was. There was no money to spare for another mouth to feed.

Cyril had so many hang-ups, it's hard to know where to start. 'I'm a typical Gemini, always of two minds,' he would tell me. True, he was gentle, kind and sentimental on the one hand, but brutal, bullying, domineering and violent on the other. At a mere 5ft 3in tall, he insisted that not one man in the world could make him feel small. 'All great men in history have been short, from Napoleon onwards,' he boasted.

He craved respectability and demanded order, but was chaotic when he was depressed. It was a warning sign if he didn't bother to clean his brushes after painting.

As a respectable working-class man Cyril would never allow himself, or me, to go out in scuffed shoes, so he cleaned and polished them until they squeaked.

Some people have a chip on their shoulder.

Like his great predecessor J.M.W. Turner, he was proud of what he had achieved in art, despite and not because of his modest roots. The working class were useless and stupid, he believed. 'There's nothing romantic about the working class,' he hissed, a view he had held since his army days.

He equally despised the snooty upper-class, public-school or university-educated 'toffs'. Those were soon to include his eldest daughter, Sylvia, and his son-in-law, Howard Dewhirst. They married soon after graduating from Keele University. 'They don't know they're born,' he would moan. He had the nasty habit of insulting and alienating potential well-heeled picture buyers. Although he was deeply uncomfortable in his own skin, he never doubted his creative gifts and intelligence. He may have had deep inferiority complexes, but these never applied to his art.

As I climbed the career ladder and became a successful PR executive, I realized we were sometimes letting ourselves down with our impoverished appearance. I remembered Cyril telling me once about the artist Walter Sickert saying: 'If you're an unsuccessful artist you should put a brass plaque outside your front door. The more unsuccessful you are, the bigger and brasher the plaque should be.' I have no idea whether Sickert actually said this, but even if we'd had a brass plaque few people would have seen it on our seventh floor door at Bevin Court.

I thought we should smarten ourselves up. I said to Cyril: 'There are lots of sales on now, and I've seen some very nice suits in the windows of Austin Reed. We have a bit of spare cash. Let's have a look.'

We went, but I could see that Cyril was immensely uncomfortable. It felt like a scene from *Are You Being Served?*, the TV comedy series about a department store. I had picked out a lovely brown tweed suit, nothing too formal. Cyril would need to have the trousers shortened.

'I'm not wearing a stiff collar,' he groaned. 'I'll find you a shirt that you'll like,' I promised. I knew he preferred those button-down American style collars. From then on, I bought all his shirts, choosing pastel shades rather than white. Cyril's Austin Reed suit was a great success and he was delighted. 'I now look like a banker,' he said proudly. 'I may not have Sickert's brass plaque on the door, but for the first time, I look like I could have money.'

SUCKER FISH, 1971
Oil on canvas, 70 x 88cm (27$\frac{1}{2}$ x 34$\frac{1}{2}$in), The Estate of Cyril Mann / courtesy of Piano Nobile, Robert Travers (Works of Art) Ltd

In Walthamstow market, a fish stall kept Cyril supplied with unusual varieties, some so ugly that customers refused to buy and eat them. In this painting, he sets this magnificent creature against a blue fruit plate and contrasting lemon.

Chapter 37

IN LOVE WITH PUNK

Towards the late 1970s Cyril suddenly professed a liking for what he considered the most significant cultural development in Britain: punk rockers. They appealed to him more than the Beatles or Stones had ever done in the past. Why? It was clearly not the raucous music, as Cyril by then was seriously deaf.

He loved their rudeness. He identified with the anti-capitalist subversion and counterculture. Above all, punks fascinated him visually, their outlandish grunge clothes, spiked dyed hair, piercings and tattoos.

'Why is nobody painting them?' he puzzled. He admired their anarchy. For years he had rejected the Beatles and Rolling Stones, only occasionally expressing a grudging admiration for Bob Dylan's lyrics.

'Punks have a significant political message,' he told me. 'They're sticking two fingers up to everyone. They're into drugs. That's why the State is terrified of them. The government don't want anyone to know how enjoyable drugs are. If they knew, nobody would do a stroke of work and just get stoned.' Cyril may have expressed such an opinion, but I knew that he himself had never experimented with opiates or drugs. He was much too scared that they would deflect him from painting.

'Punks look different from anyone we've seen before,' said Cyril. 'Portrait painters should be at their easels, recording what they look like for the future. For once, I regret not being a portrait painter.'

He repeated his lament to his wealthy artist friend, Zsuzsi Roboz. Unlike Cyril, she specialized in portraits, but these tended to be of famous actors, dancers and musicians. Zsuzsi took note and befriended some punks who looked like proverbial fish out of water when they turned up at one of her posh private views.

No artist, as far as I know, has done justice in painting to the punk movement. Why not? For the same age-old reason: art buyers were not attracted to the subject matter. There was not enough money in it.

Chapter 38

ENDGAME

The fact that my marriage broke down after twenty years was my failing and I blame myself, absolutely. Not only was I exhausted and desperate to enjoy myself with people of my own age, I had lost patience and hated every minute I had to spend with Cyril. I loathed his despair, ravings, threats, agonies and frustrations.

After we moved out of Bevin Court and into our own house, my career in PR took off, and I began to earn a proper living. Soon, my higher income enabled us to move out of Walthamstow and into a much larger house in Leyton, also in East London.

While Cyril had never wanted another child, he kept to his word that he would never deny me a baby when I thought the time was right. He was thrilled and delighted when Amanda was born. 'I've always dreamt of having a brown-eyed baby,' he said. He was an excellent and caring father. I made sure the baby didn't cause too many distractions, first by using a baby minder nearby, then employing a full-time nanny when my career became ever more demanding, as I travelled around the world on business. But we never had a live-in nanny as none would have put up with Cyril's moods and rages.

For the first time Cyril had the ideal set-up for painting. The large sun-filled room he used as a studio in the front of our Victorian house was almost as big as our entire Bevin Court flat.

Cyril was doing many self-portraits during this time, seeming to relish depicting himself in old age and, like Rembrandt, looking increasingly decrepit and sad. When he was not busy painting, he tended our large back garden at the back, growing nearly all our vegetables as well as the flowers – chrysanthemums, delphiniums, roses – used in his late still life paintings.

AMANDA WITH RAG DOLL IN SUNLIGHT, 1973
Oil on canvas, 94 x 71cm (37 x 28in), Collection Renske Mann

Thirty years separate Cyril's portraits of his two daughters, Sylvia (1940–2006) painted in 1943 (see page 120) and Amanda in 1973. With the painting of his second child, he was more interested in the dynamic effects of light than in rendering her features. Both children suffered greatly for his art.

These more comfortable circumstances should have made for contentment, but gradually Cyril's resentment grew. He found it hard to feel any gratitude towards me. He hated to be 'the taker' in our relationship. For the first time in our lives, he minded relying on me financially. He kept asking me: 'What's your motive, Renske? Why should you want to help me?' I was no longer prepared to kowtow to his unreasonable demands: that I should be ready to discuss his work with him whenever he wanted. We had hours of heated conversation and tiresome arguments. At weekends, when I was exhausted and wanted to relax, he demanded that I should follow his whims and go out to the British Museum or National Gallery. He was lonely, spending most of his days painting at home. All I longed for was to curl up with a book.

At first Cyril thought my relationship with an old girlfriend was a joke. He was never jealous, nor did it sexually excite him, as it might have some men. 'I want to paint you together and outdo Courbet,' he enthused. The nineteenth-century French artist had famously painted some sensuous female double nudes. In preparation, Cyril made dozens of drawings of my girlfriend and me, but never proceeded to turn them into oils. He just lacked the energy.

'At the bottom, you're normal, Renske,' he kept reassuring me and himself. My girlfriend occasionally stayed with us, deepening the cracks in our already fractious marriage. Gradually I began to love her more than I did him. It's just as well my affair wasn't with a man. The result, literally, would have been murder.

ECCE HOMO, 1978
Oil on canvas, 136 x 103cm (53¹/₂ x 40¹/₂in), Private Collection

This is almost Cyril's last self-portrait. He died a year later, mentally unstable but defiant and with undimmed creative energy. Against doctors' orders, he is smoking again. In this portrait he sees himself as Jesus Christ, crucified by a lifetime lack of success. The two earlier self-portraits that flank him symbolize the thieves, crucified alongside Christ.

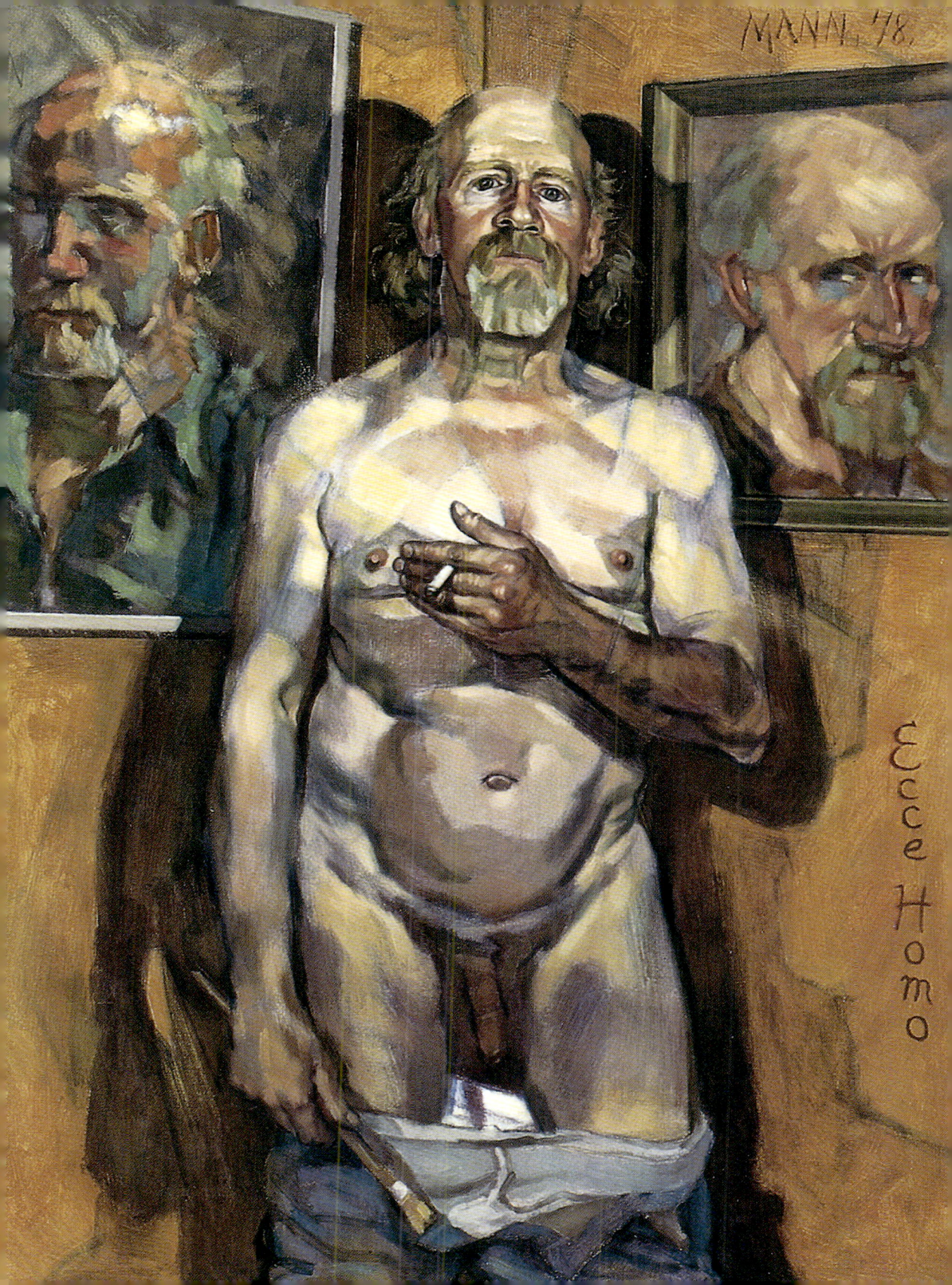

MANA '78.

Ecce Homo

Chapter 39

CRUNCH YEAR

I buckled under the strain of caring for Cyril and Amanda while struggling with my all-consuming job as PR director of footcare company Scholl. I should have taken it easy after Amanda was born, but without paid maternity leave, I was back at my desk days after coming home from hospital. I went on to study for a degree with the Open University and five years on – now aged thirty-six – I had notched up several OU credits towards my BA degree.

Bored with the trappings of my professional success, I began to take for granted a generous salary and expenses, my name and title on my office door, the new company car, and tea tray delivered to my desk in the afternoon. I even had the occasional use of our company plane for press visits to the Scholl sandal factory in Austria. I was paying the price physically and emotionally, and without either Cyril or me realizing it, I was close to burnout.

I longed for a peaceful, less demanding life. The answer, I believed, could lie in teaching. With my Open University qualifications I could qualify in two years.

With Cyril's reluctant approval – he had hated teaching years ago and couldn't understand why I should want to give up my well-paid career – I applied for a full grant, but was quickly turned down because I was female.

In desperation, I asked Bryan Magee, our Labour MP for Leyton in the Harold Wilson government, to take up the cudgels on my behalf. The Hansard entry, entitled Student Grants, 13 January 1975, records his address to the House and his reference to my predicament.

Bryan Magee, for all his efforts, failed to persuade Parliament to change the rules and allow me to enter a teacher's training college on a full grant. I felt deflated, a spent force, and abandoned the idea of switching careers. Looking back, I'm glad I did so and carried on working in PR and not only for material benefits. Had I left the profession in 1975, I might never have met Marion Mathews, my future love and partner, through work.

After losing his seat in the 1976 parliamentary election, Magee went on to have a distinguished career as a university professor, a music and theatre critic, and author of several internationally acclaimed books on philosophy and on the composer Richard Wagner. He also hosted a television series interviewing British philosophers.

I met Bryan again after thirty-eight years, when he gave a lecture during a Wagner Ring Cycle in Longborough, Gloucestershire. 'Long ago, you were our MP in Leyton,'

SUNLIT INTERIOR WITH WRITING DESK, 1978
Oil on board, 60 x 45cm (23½ x 17¾in), The Estate of Cyril Mann / courtesy of Piano Nobile, Robert Travers (Works of Art) Ltd

The morning sun enters through the side window, bouncing off the glass panes of our mahogany writing desk. Cyril opens its doors to maximize reflections. He's never had or wanted a studio. If something inspired him, he wanted to paint it straightaway. Our entire house was at his disposal.

I reminded him, strolling to his desk. 'You may remember me and my husband, the artist Cyril Mann? You visited us at home.'

Bryan was flabbergasted but delighted. He recognized me, but failed to recall the details of our case, which he had argued so cogently as an MP in the House. 'You look very well, are you happy?' he asked. 'I am, yes I am,' I replied truthfully. I never saw him again. He died in 2019, aged eighty-nine.

RENSKE IN SUNLIGHT, 1966
Oil on canvas, 82 x 65cm (32¼ x 25½in), The Estate of Cyril Mann / courtesy of Piano Nobile, Robert Travers (Works of Art) Ltd

Life was hard as I grew up and built a career in public relations. It didn't take long to realize that we could not make a living from Cyril's paintings. He left it to me to find exhibition opportunities. He refused to apply to galleries himself. I worry a lot but know that Cyril loves me. He has provided me with our own home in Walthamstow.

Chapter 40

THE END

Friends had pointed out for years that Cyril had severe mental problems. But I was in denial, trying to ignore his tantrums and putting up with him. When Glen Robson, a friend and collector of Cyril's pictures, stayed with us, he could hear Cyril's ranting and raving for hours through the night. Next morning he said to me, 'I couldn't stand it for twenty minutes; how have you put up with it for twenty years?'

Now I knew our days together were numbered. I had reached the end of my tether, and Cyril, realizing this, was in despair.

In 1979, as we were approaching the twentieth anniversary of our first meeting at Kingsway Day College, Cyril became unwell. A side wall of our house, three floors high, urgently needed repointing. Try as I might, I couldn't persuade Cyril to get a team of men in to do this. Instead, he insisted on doing this incredibly hard job by himself: climbing up and down scaffolding with heavy buckets of mortar mix, while scraping out the old mortar first and breathing in clouds of dust. 'A fool and his money are soon parted,' he insisted angrily. 'Ol' Mike wouldn't let other fools help him with his ceiling in the Sistine Chapel.'

Cyril was covered in dust and exhausted for weeks on end. I didn't realize how sick he was. Almost inevitably, he had a heart attack, but not a major one, and after he finished repointing our house, he made a swift recovery. By then it was December 1979. He was sixty-eight. I had just turned forty. Our age difference, which had seemed so unimportant in our early days together, had created a huge chasm. He was ready to put his feet up. I felt my life had just begun. Amanda, now aged eleven, was at boarding school in Eastbourne on an open scholarship.

Then I started to feel unwell, too. I was chain smoking again to steady my nerves. I couldn't cope with Cyril's fury and insults. My girlfriend had walked out a few months earlier, filling me with despair. I began to get very scared of Cyril.

One night, after an abusive row, I fled – with Cyril asleep – and drove like a madwoman to our old friends, Michael and Sylvia Leibson. They were deeply concerned at my fragile mental and physical state and put me to bed in a spare room to sleep. When I finally went back to our house just before Christmas 1979 – exactly twenty years since we met – Cyril had seriously deteriorated, mentally and physically. I wouldn't – couldn't – even consider going back to him. I felt drained, exhausted and totally spent. I promised to support him financially for as long as he lived. He could see our Amanda whenever he wanted, provided he was fit and sane enough.

I was deaf to his desperate pleas. He was heartbroken and his anguish caused an immediate and severe mental breakdown. Wandering the streets, ranting and raving to all and sundry, he was arrested and sectioned in Claybury Mental Hospital.

What saved me was my relationship with Marion Mathews, whom I had met at work three years earlier in 1976. It had started tentatively. We enjoyed being together, promising each other to be loving friends and friendly lovers. When I was going through my traumas with Cyril, she was away at a conference abroad. I couldn't contact her to tell her that I had run away in the middle of the night, much as Mary had done in the early 1950s.

The Leibsons were the only friends I could turn to. I stayed in their house for a few nights until Marion returned. She agreed I could stay with her, but not immediately, as she would be with her mother in Woodford over Christmas and New Year. I decided to take Amanda to my parents and family in Holland.

On my return to London in the New Year, I telephoned a neighbour in Leyton to ask how Cyril was coping. She told me he had been in a coma for a week in Whipps Cross Hospital. He had had another, this time major, heart attack. I rushed to the hospital where I found Cyril unconscious.

Shocked and grief stricken, I sat crying by his bed, stroking his hand. Did he know I was there? He looked angry, terrifyingly angry, as he did in many of his late self-portraits. A doctor assured me he could not be in pain. Minutes after my arrival, he seemed to wake for a few seconds. Then, with a sigh and us holding hands, he died quietly and silently of heart failure. It was 7 January 1980, almost exactly twenty years after we first met.

I couldn't face going back to our house in Leyton, but Glen Robson volunteered to go and found a letter among various documents and bits of writing strewn about, written by Cyril in response to a letter received from me after neighbours informed me that they had seen 'unknown visitors, leaving our home with arms full of paintings'. Desperate for company, Cyril had welcomed anyone who cared to visit, and some people took advantage of that.

My Dear Love,

I received your letter this morning and was afraid to open it for I was so filled with foreboding, which was justified on reading the content. When I saw the word solicitor, I knew my last bit of hope was gone. I'm not going to get upset for it won't do me any good – harm in fact.

This in a way will be my last love letter to you. I do love you, Renske, (oh Sweetheart) and always shall. You can cease to love but you will never get rid of mine. In all my pictures the evidence is there and will remain for people to see and realize. You have been a dear and wonderful wife, giving me all and putting me first always. I have been aware of it and have never taken it for granted. Thank you for everything and all the happiness that went with it. I shall always be grateful. I'm not bitter or angry even though you have truly broken my heart.

Every day I realize more the reason for taking the step you have. It couldn't have been an easy decision of you but I now see that it was necessary and that you were really unhappy at home with me and had to take the final step. So, love, don't please feel guilty or self-reproachful for there is no need. In all things I want is for you to be happy and to realize yourself and live fully. You've done your twenty years chores on me. Now think of yourself. You've earned it. So I say God Bless, take care of yourself. Remember my heart and any help you may need is yours to call upon at any time….

Cyril's last letter to me is quoted verbatim. I have kept it in his archive. It gave me back the will – and the courage – to live. I believe that was what he intended it to do.

Chapter 41

AFTERMATH

Sixty years after Cyril and I married, I'm still mystified as to why I should have fallen so quickly and deeply in love with him. I was oblivious of risks. Within weeks I had recklessly promised to devote my life to him. Was it fate? Looking back, the portents were there long before I left Dordrecht for England.

I desperately wanted to go to art school, but my parents decided otherwise. Earning a living as a shorthand-typist was less precarious, they said.

In a huff, I went for a walk around our nearby park to let off steam, when the park warden tapped on my shoulder. 'What's upset you?' he asked, spotting my teenage sulk. I told him about my parents' refusal to send me to art school. 'Don't worry,' he said, looking into my eyes. 'You'll have all the art you could want in your life. You'll meet and marry an artist. You'll know him the minute you see him.'

The park warden was psychic, he explained. My life was already mapped out, he told me. 'I can see your future husband standing behind you.' Minutes later: 'No, that can't be him. He's too old. That must be his father.'

Years went by. I met several young, talented artists of my own age without a flicker of interest on my part. Now I believe that the park warden's prediction stayed with me subliminally, as it were, until the moment I stood on tiptoe and saw Cyril's back through the classroom window. Something clicked in my mind. The minute I saw him, I never doubted we were destined for each other.

I told Cyril about the prediction, expecting him to laugh, but no. '*Que sera, sera,*' he said wistfully. 'What will be, will be.'

My friendship with Cyril's first wife, Mary, and their daughter, Sylvia, continued until they died years later. Mary was in her eighties, but Sylvia passed away in her sixties, a few months after her mother.

Our daughter, Amanda, has followed in her father's footsteps and is also a fine artist.

Marion and I have lived together ever since Cyril died. We became civil partners in 2004. After renovating a derelict dairy in Holland Park, we established a gallery in 1985. We ran it on almost a charitable basis, charging the lowest commission of any gallery in London.

At the Holland Gallery, we gave talented artists the opportunity to show their work in a sympathetic, professional environment, one that Cyril himself would have loved. I am convinced that Cyril will one day be recognized as one of the 'greats' of British art. Shortly after we met, I promised him I would never stop fighting for him and his art. That promise still holds six decades later.

ALLOTMENTS, WALTHAMSTOW, ON A SUNNY DAY, 1968
Oil on board, 51 x 61cm (20 x 24 in), The Estate of Cyril Mann / courtesy of Piano Nobile, Robert Travers (Works of Art) Ltd

Cyril was never happier than when wandering around the allotments on his doorstep in Lynmouth Road. I can still see him kicking off his muddy shoes at the door and rushing upstairs to paint. 'Ideally, I'd love to live on a farm, far away from people but with you by my side to paint,' he confessed. I shuddered at the thought, but never let on.

SELF-PORTRAIT, *c.*1950
Oil on board, 49.5 x 44.5cm (19½ x 17½in) The Estate of Cyril Mann / courtesy of Piano Nobile,
Robert Travers (Works of Art) Ltd

Cyril is nearly forty in this self-portrait and his life is about to take a turn for the worse.
Mary, his first wife, runs out of patience and decides to leave and start a new life, taking their
daughter, Sylvia.

CYRIL MANN (1911–80)
A BRIEF HISTORY OF THE ARTIST

1911

Born 28 May in Paddington, London, third child of William and Gertrude Mann, both originally from Nottingham.

1914

Father, William Mann, is conscripted into the army at the outbreak of the First World War.

1918

Parents return to Nottingham. After an honorable discharge with shell shock, William enters the Saxondale Hospital in Sneinton (the city's psychiatric hospital) and remains there until his death in 1938. Gertrude – known as Gertie – is left to raise their daughter and three sons on a small war pension.

1923

Aged 12, Cyril is the youngest boy to win a scholarship to the Nottingham School of Art.

1925

Leaves school and fails his entrance exam to become an office clerk at Boots the Chemists. He then works elsewhere as a clerk for a year.

1927

Travels to Canada to become a missionary.

1928–31

Abandons religious life and works as a miner, logger, travelling salesman and printer. Virtually isolated from the civilized world on the Alaskan border, the beauty of the landscape inspires him to start painting again.

1932

Meets Arthur Lismer, a Sheffield-born painter and member of the Canadian 'Group of Seven', and is influenced by the work of these post-Impressionist painters. Lismer advises the young man to return to England to continue his art education.

1933–4

Returns to England and settles in London. In the depth of the Depression years, unemployed and often close to starvation, he specializes in watercolours of Paddington and Maida Vale.

1935

Meets the Revd Oliver Fielding Clarke, leading light in the Toc H youth organization, who introduces the young artist to Erica Marx, well-known arts patron. A trust fund is set up enabling him to study at the Royal Academy (RA) Schools, where he is admitted that year.

1938

Leaves RA Schools to continue studying in Paris, supported by Erica Marx. Meets Mary Jervis-Read.

1939

Returns to London before outbreak of Second World War and marries Mary.

1940

Birth of daughter Sylvia. Serves as a gunner in the Royal Artillery until the end of the war.

1946

Becomes a conscientious objector when conscripted after the war. His case goes before a tribunal. He suffers extreme ill health and stomach ulcers.

1947

Appointed art lecturer at the London County Council Central School of Art and continues to teach there until 1949.

1948

Takes part in exhibition 'Artists of Fame and Promise' at the Wildenstein Gallery.

1950–55

Appointed lecturer at Kingsway Day College and the Sir John Cass College, specializing in the technology of painting. Separates from his wife Mary. Exhibitions during this period include Park Row Gallery of the Midland Group of Artists and Designers, Nottingham, and at various London galleries, including two-man show with Anne Estelle Rice at the Brook Street Gallery, mixed shows at the Hanover Gallery, the East End Academy at the Whitechapel Gallery, and several shows at the Archer Gallery in Notting Hill.

1956

Moves into flat 108, Bevin Court, a 'Brutalist' high-rise social housing block in Islington.

1958

Designs and works on large sculpture commission for a crest on Heath House, a manor house in Hopton Heath, Shropshire.

1959

His mother, Gertrude Mann, dies in a Nottingham nursing home after outliving her husband, daughter and two of her three sons. Depressed and in bad health, Cyril meets Dutch-Indonesian Renske Mann a week before Christmas.

1960

After an emergency operation for a perforated ulcer, Cyril has a serious nervous breakdown. On recovery, he marries Renske, who persuades him to give up teaching and concentrate full-time on his painting, promising to share what she earns with him.

1963

One-man show at St Martin's Gallery, near St Martin's Lane.

1964

One-man show at Rawinski Gallery, near Carnaby Street, Soho.

1965

Paintings selected for opening show at the Alwin Gallery, Brook Street, Mayfair.

1966

Joins and exhibits with the Contemporary Portrait Society. He and Renske move to Walthamstow in East London.

1967

Two-man show at Alwin Gallery.

1968

Third exhibition at the Alwin Gallery. Birth of second daughter, Amanda Renske.

1969

Moves to Leyton, East London, having use of a large studio space for the first time. He goes out to paint local scenes, including landscapes of Epping Forest and landmarks such as the gas cooling towers, canals and culverts.

1970

Shows with Contemporary Portrait Society at Upper Grosvenor Gallery and has various private exhibitions in the Canonbury home of Dr Michael Leibson and his sculptor wife, Sylvia, his patrons for many years.

1978

Exhibition at the Ogle Gallery, Eastbourne. Starts having severe physical and mental health problems, culminating in being sectioned and admitted to Claybury Mental Hospital. Renske leaves but continues to support him financially.

1980

Dies in Whipps Cross Hospital of heart failure on 7 January.

APPENDIX: HOW IT BEGAN

By Liz Hodgkinson

I first met Renske and her partner, journalist Marion Mathews, at their home in West London in 1981, when I was working for the *Daily Mail* and Renske was PR director for Scholl, the foot and sandal specialists. Our paths crossed frequently and our friendship continued over the years.

In 1982 and with great daring, Renske and Marion bought a derelict dairy in Holland Park, now one of the most desirable addresses in the country. They set about converting the shop into an art gallery and refurbishing the flat above. Their ambitious project took three years and every penny they could muster.

The old Holland Dairy became the Holland Gallery with Renske and Marion as co-directors. It had long been Renske's dream to help unknown gifted artists, like her late husband, with a first foot on the exhibition ladder. The gallery quickly turned into a popular social hub, attracting hundreds of applications from painters and sculptors.

Because both women worked full-time – Renske as freelance PR consultant based at the gallery – they could run their enterprise on an almost charitable basis. By then I was divorced and had moved to nearby Notting Hill. I supported the gallery and bought pictures at private views to adorn my own new home.

As I came to know Renske better, I learned about her unusual relationship with her late husband and saw Cyril's paintings in their flat above the gallery. I knew that Renske and Cyril had a daughter, Amanda, who was the same age as my older son Tom. I also knew that their twenty-year marriage had ended badly but was unaware of the details.

When Renske Mann began posting Cyril Mann's paintings on Facebook, I immediately wanted to know more about these wonderful artworks and the painter who had created them. Other followers were also fascinated by Renske's posts and thought the same. Gradually the idea emerged that these intriguing vignettes might be expanded into a memoir.

In particular, I wanted to understand why a young girl on the verge of adulthood should have fallen passionately in love with an irascible, poverty-stricken artist thirty years her senior. Was it the art, the man, or a mixture of both? Wherein lay the attraction? Gradually, as more revelations appeared, the whole thing expanded into a most unusual true-life story.

At the time the Facebook posts began, we had been friends and professional colleagues for nearly forty years.

I offered to edit Renske's story and gradually a story of love, hope, despair, mental illness, failure, rejection, extreme poverty and intermittent success emerged from the random memories.

Although Cyril Mann's art features prominently, the book is also the tale of a remarkable woman who supported a husband three decades her senior as muse, model and chief money earner. It tells the story of what it was really like to be married to a prodigiously talented artist whose unstable, erratic personality made him difficult to live with. Renske clearly had a deep and unusual understanding of her husband's art and had also been his model.

I was an extremely lucky editor in that Renske had kept much of the archive material that makes the book so rich and rewarding a read. She seemed to have thrown nothing away, allowing us to fill in the tantalizing gaps in her Facebook postings.

Within weeks of meeting, Renske had promised Cyril that she would devote her life to him. For twenty years they shared her earnings, so that he could concentrate on his art without financial worries. She fulfilled her promise at a time when it was almost unheard of for a wife, especially one so much younger, to be the main breadwinner.

Eight years after Cyril's death, art dealer Dr Robert Travers came across his paintings almost by accident and was immediately convinced that he had chanced upon an unsung genius of the twentieth century.

With Robert's expertise, Cyril's reputation has gone from strength to strength. His pictures have been sold into major public and private collections worldwide. Several exhibitions have been held over the years in Robert's gallery, Piano Nobile. A monograph on Cyril's life and art was written by the *Times* art critic John Russell Taylor and the paintings began to fetch significant sums.

Articles and reviews began appearing in art journals, mainstream magazines and newspapers. In 2013, a commemorative plaque was placed on Bevin Court, the Islington council flats where Cyril and Renske had started their married life and where he had done many of his finest paintings It was the first time that a social housing block had been graced with a plaque.

Renske's autobiography provides astonishing insights into the mind of a great British artist. It will appeal not just to an art-loving public, but to readers who enjoy a rattling good tale and one which follows the ups and downs of one of the greatest love stories in the twentieth century.

POSTSCRIPT

By Mark Hudson

The wheel of artistic fashion turned many times through the nearly sixty years of Cyril Mann's career, with abstraction, conceptualism and figuration going in and out of favour. Throughout these changes in taste, Cyril stood apart, not merely impervious or hostile to changing trends, but often seeming to exist outside conventional artistic time.

Leafing through the pictures in this book, we can't fail to be struck by Cyril's extraordinary capacity to get what was in front of him down on canvas, board or paper with a sense of absolute conviction. That capacity, rare enough in any era, tends to arouse a degree of suspicion in an age when art has focused on so many other things. The painter who can make things look the way they are generally understood to be, who can do just about anything they want with paint, must be, conventional logic has it, a 'conservative artist' at best, or a purveyor of pastiche and, at worst, a fraud. None of these notions come close to applying to Cyril Mann.

You can search in vain through an oeuvre encompassing expressionistic streetscapes, proto-pop still lifes, latter-day Impressionism and apparently very traditional portraiture for the faintest trace of manner or stylization. Where there are touches of the topographical and the illustrative they feel entirely deliberate – as in *Tower Block and Cottages, Walthamstow*, 1969 (page 56). A close examination of Cyril's portraits leaves you wondering if the notion of 'traditional' has any real meaning.

The British critic in 1965 who appeared bemused by Cyril's faith in observation from nature in the age of 'kinetics' and pop art clearly hadn't seen his solid-shadow paintings (an excellent example on page 49). With their strong outlines and emblematic colours, these works would have felt more 'of the moment', though they were painted a good ten years earlier. Indeed, while these paintings anticipate both pop art and Michael Craig Martin's twenty-first-century conceptual realism – the latter by some decades – they were created, in 1952–3, before the apparently very conventional, yet extremely impressive *Portrait of Sylvia*, 1957 (page 61), a work which might at first glance have been painted at any time over the preceding hundred years.

This image of Mann's elder daughter as a slightly sulky seventeen-year-old is predated by a portrait of Sylvia as a baby, painted fifteen years earlier, which feels – counter-intuitively – more modern with its hint of post-Impressionism, though it's equally forceful in bringing a human presence before us through paint.

Jumping forward to 1963, we see Cyril evolving his own kind of kitchen-sink Cubism in *Modern Venus* (page 51), but one determined entirely by light, in a work that ushers in his final phase, in which space and form are constructed through broad brushstrokes corresponding to flickering flashes of light.

Since van Gogh we've come to accept that the artist's real subject isn't the reality in front of them, but their inner vision of that reality. Cyril, on the other hand, in contrast to everything we might have expected of him – and he suffered quite as many personal challenges as Vincent – seems out to efface his own presence. With very few exceptions, Cyril – like Constable before him and another of his great heroes, Cezanne – aspires, we feel, to act as a dispassionate conductor for objective reality with the subject itself determining the final appearance of the work. Even in the teeth of outright mania, Cyril appears in control as an artist – if in nothing else.

The works where I feel most in Cyril's metaphysical shoes, most behind his eyes in that process, are the paintings of bomb-damaged London, completed mostly between 1948 and 1950, where he worked looking directly into the sun. *St Paul's from Moor Lane* (page 114) is a great London picture, hugely evocative of its time, with its battered walls, field of ruins, people hurrying to work, and the muggy silhouette of that majestic dome rearing into a yellow smog-laden sky. But even more powerful in my view, because they are less tied to topography and historical association, and therefore rawer and more universal in their impact, are works such as *Sunburst* (1948), *View of Spitalfields* (1948) or in this book *Sunlit Landscape* (page 64), which while painted as far away as Rickmansworth is very much part of the series.

These are London paintings which, like the best of the School of London painters' works, step beyond the notion of a physical locality; they are works which overwhelm the viewer, the dimensions of the canvas and, we feel, the process of looking itself with the physical stuff of overpowering transcendent light.

INDEX

Page numbers in *italics* refer to illustrations. Page numbers followed by 'n' refer to captions.

PICTURE CREDITS

All pictures of artworks and archival photographs are Courtesy PIANO NOBILE, Robert Travers (Works of Art) Ltd. or from the Collection of Renske Mann with the exception of the following:

page 10 NPG 6931 © Cyril Mann Estate c/o Robert Travers (Works of Art) Ltd London / National Portrait Gallery, London

page 72 both images © www.ianvisits.com

page 88 Ben Uri Collection © Cyril Mann Estate c/o Robert Travers (Works of Art) Ltd

page 106 Lebrecht Music & Arts / Alamy Stock Photo

page 131 artist copyright © Zsuzsi Roboz courtesy PIANO NOBILE, Robert Travers (Works of Art) Ltd

ACKNOWLEDGEMENTS

I owe this memoir to Liz Hodgkinson, author/journalist and friend, who has guided me every step of the way, transforming my life story with Cyril into a coherent book. I thank Liz for generously providing her superb writing and editing skills honed in Fleet Street. Without her, I doubt if this book would ever have seen the light of day.

I also thank Mark Hudson, prize-winning author and art critic, for helping at a later stage to refine the book, writing the introduction and the postscript.

I want to thank all my now mostly absent friends for their lifelong help and patience, not made easy by Cyril in his lifetime.

Among the most important are the late Dr Mike and Sylvia Leibson, and my best friend and mentor in life and business, Phyllis Bowman. I shall never forget Dr David and Hilda Hardisty, Stewart and Thelma Shepley and many others who collected Cyril's paintings when they could ill afford them.

More recently, I thank John Russell Taylor, author and *Times* art critic, who wrote Cyril's monograph: *The Sun is God: The Life and Work of Cyril Mann*. He and his partner, Ying Yeung Li, shared a friendship with another wonderful supporter, the late Zsuzsi Roboz, a soulmate and Cyril's art companion.

I thank Dr Robert Travers of Piano Nobile Gallery, who has looked after the Cyril Mann estate for the past thirty years with great sensitivity while leaving no stone unturned in promoting his works. He is now ably assisted by his eldest son, Matthew, and daughter Roberta, who have grown up surrounded by Cyril's paintings and share his enthusiasm.

I'm grateful to Cyril for giving me our beautiful daughter, Amanda, who has followed in his footsteps and is now also a talented artist.

Finally, my deep gratitude goes to my better half and partner, Marion Mathews. She has put up with my obsession with Cyril and his art for more than forty years, which can't have been easy for her.